A Dog's Life

MARTIN CLUNES

A Dog's Life

HODDER &
STOUGHTON

First published in Great Britain in 2008 by Hodder & Stoughton
An Hachette Livre UK company

1

Copyright © 2008 ITV Productions Limited and Buffalo Pictures Limited

The right of Martin Clunes to be identified as the
Author of the Work has been asserted by him in accordance
with the Copyright, Designs and Patents Act 1988.

A CIP catalogue record for this title is available from the British Library

Hardback ISBN 978 0 340 97704 0
Trade Paperback ISBN 978 0 340 97774 3

Typeset in Plantin Light by Hewer Text UK Ltd, Edinburgh
Printed and bound in the UK by CPI Mackays, Chatham ME5 8TD

Hodder & Stoughton policy is to use papers that are natural, renewable
and recyclable products and made from wood grown in sustainable forests.
The logging and manufacturing processes are expected to conform
to the environmental regulations of the country of origin.

Hodder & Stoughton Ltd
338 Euston Road
London NW1 3BH

www.hodder.co.uk

To my mum
Daphne Gillian Clunes
4 July 1928 – 17 September 2007
Who didn't really care for dogs, but let us have one anyway.
x

Contents

18 Behaving Obediently   269
19 Tails from the Green Room   281
20 The Darker Side of Love   297
21 The Day the Dogs Ran Free   311
22 For the Best   331

    Acknowledgments   341
    Picture Acknowledgments   343

Introduction

There is a fact generally acknowledged, dear reader, that a man is not a man without a dog.

I have always been a pushover when it comes to dogs – something my own dogs worked out a long time ago. If a crowd gathers in Port Isaac to watch us shoot a scene in *Doc Martin*, I always go up to chat to the people who have brought their dogs along. I genuinely enjoy hearing about them. Some people borrow dogs, knowing that they'll almost certainly get to speak to me if they do. Talking about their dogs makes people relax – it's much easier than nervously asking for an autograph. The director of *Doc Martin*, Ben Bolt, once told me that he'd worked with an actor who, whenever there was a break in the shooting, would make a beeline for the nearest blonde in the crowd. 'Whereas you,' he said, 'always go for the nearest dog!'

When my daughter Emily was at that stage when she took two naps of a couple of hours each during the day, I remember clearly the jolt of elation I always felt when I saw her again after her rest. It was a repeat of the feeling I got as a schoolboy when the girl I had the crush on came into the classroom. I have to confess that I get a similar, perhaps diluted feeling when I catch sight of certain dogs and most puppies. There are some dogs that I just have to go over and touch.

Emily is the same. When she was little, we had a Saturday morning ritual of going to a local street market to buy old ladies' watercolours and odd bits and pieces. It would take us forever to get down all the stalls because we kept stopping to meet all the dogs. I taught her from a very early age to let a dog smell your hand before you touch it. Emily and I both go, 'Aaaah,' at the same type of dog: of no particular breed, slightly grey jowls, generally a bitch. They're not necessarily slender or muscular, and a bandanna will always do the trick.

I'm curious about dogs, about what makes them tick. I enjoy trying to engage with them and love hearing stories about what they've got up to. Most of all, I like chuckling them around the chops. I don't mind being licked on the face but I particularly like being licked in the ear, especially by a cocker spaniel's pointy tongue, or having my toes licked. I take real pleasure in a dog's excitement and enthusiasm for life and its unquestioning friendliness. The physical contact between man and dog can be so satisfying when you stroke, pat or chuckle them. I particularly admire their chests, always big enough for a good rub. Otherwise, I'm jealous of their snouts because they're whiskery and seem to me a pleasing thing to own. Occasionally I think I've even dreamed that I have one myself.

I know it's important not to anthropomorphise or project human values on to dogs but I can't help feeling that they're just little hairy people with four legs and nice long noses going about their business. I find that terribly attractive and funny.

I love getting up close and personal with a dog, rubbing my cheek against the side of their face. And there's nothing like the smell of the top of a puppy's head or behind a grown dog's ear. Behind the ear is always warm and smells quite sensual. I've always thought that if you were going to extract an essential oil from a dog, it would come either from there or from the side of their snouts.

I've yet to meet a dog that I dislike. Occasionally I feel sorry for a dog, if it's over-bred or over-pampered and stuffed in a handbag, but that's only because the owner has removed the dog's essential 'dogness'. That's what's important to me. What I call 'dogness' is a spirit, a general celebration of life. Everything is full of festivity, whether it's getting ready for a walk, being fed or greeting their owner in the morning. Who else can be relied on to be that excited about seeing you first thing, day in day out? To get that amount of pleasure out of life seems hugely enviable to me.

I

Something about Mary

London and Dorset

*'If forced to make a choice, my dog among dogs
would have to be the cocker spaniel'*

If asked, I'd find it hard to pick a favourite breed. A dog is a dog. Even the hairless ones. But if I was forced to make a choice, my dog among dogs would have to be the cocker spaniel. I always say there are two breeds of spaniel: working cockers and bone-idle cockers. Ours definitely belong to the second group. My family owns two, Mary and Tina, and although they've given us a lot of heartache they've also given us an extraordinary amount of pleasure. I'm inordinately proud of both of them, but the most important dog in my life would have to be Mary Elizabeth, 'the first born'.

Philippa and I were newly married and there were two holes in our life together: one was dog-shaped, the other child-shaped. We knew we could fill the dog-shaped hole immediately, but the other was less certain; so we began our search for a puppy. That's when we first met Mary, a two-week-old golden cocker spaniel.

7

There was no question about which breed we were going to get. Growing up in rural Surrey, Philippa had always had cockers in the house and indeed had had them imprinted on her since early childhood. After Emily and Emma, who were both run over, came Dizzy, who survived to the grand old age of eighteen. I actually met Dizzy a number of times when I first knew Philippa. She (Dizzy, that is) was sweet, kindly and rather blind. Halfway or so through Dizzy's life the family thought it would be a nice idea to get a friend for her, so a puppy called Poppy was procured. But the two dogs never connected, and lived life adjacently to one another with little or no interaction.

From my past, the only spaniel I had known was my aunt's: a black one called Sambo, who obligingly let himself be used as a ball in a game of catch played by my cousins. But I was happy to go along with whatever Philippa chose – any dog would be good enough for me. As far as I'm concerned they're all great, although some breeds suit certain situations better than others. You wouldn't want to put a lab in a handbag or go shooting with a shitapoo. At the time our lives were divided between a London flat overlooking the river in Blackfriars and a Georgian former vicarage in Dorset, so we needed a medium-sized dog that would travel well. Spaniels have a particularly good reputation for being good with both adults and children. A spaniel perfectly fitted the bill.

The Kennel Club website shows all their registered breeders across the country. We logged on, clicked on the puppy sales register, typed in the breed, then clicked on the south-east of England. We checked down the list until we found a litter of five two-week-old black-and-gold cocker spaniel pups in Kent. We contacted the breeder, who sent us a photo of them – all flat-nosed with recently opened button-black eyes and so young that their ears still stuck up.

A few weeks later we drove to a housing estate near Ashford. As we walked up the path we could hear the sound of barking on the other side of the front door. Inside, it was cocker heaven. You could have sworn no one else lived there but the dogs. There was very little furniture, but no mess. The downstairs rooms were divided off with baby-gates so that the puppies and adults would be kept apart. In the kitchen the mother, aunt and cousins of the litter rushed towards us. The mother, Miss Pollyanna Pickles, was a fine-looking black bitch – if I can say that – compactly built with a kind-looking face and a well-proportioned body. Pleased to see you, like all spaniels they jumped up on their hind legs with their front legs open like arms, even though they're not meant to bend that way.

There are few sights more irresistible than a cocker spaniel puppy. Five of them romped around a wooden whelping box lined with newspaper. They skittered up to us to investigate, tumbling over one another in their curiosity. I'd have been happy with any of the three bitches but Philippa was drawn to the smallest, most demure of them. I couldn't fault her either. The Kennel

Club warns potential puppy owners against choosing the most timid in a litter, but she was just what we were looking for: a golden bitch and the prettiest of the bunch. When she sat, she made a particular little golden triangle shape that we still see sometimes. If we go on a walk and she doesn't want to come with us, we'll look back and way in the distance we'll see that same golden triangle stubbornly refusing to move.

A couple of weeks later, when we returned to pick up our puppy, now weaned, the breeder asked us what we were going to call her. On her pedigree, she was named China Cowdray Red.

'Mary,' I replied firmly. I'd always wanted a dog called Mary, and this one was such a Mary.

I noticed the raised eyebrow. 'You're not really going to call her Mary, are you?' she asked, lemon-lipped.

'Well, yeah, I think so.' I said. 'Aren't we, Mare?'

'Not Mare!' A slight shudder went through her.

I've never called her 'Mare' since.

Back in the car, with Mary curled up like a tiny croissant on a cushion on Philippa's lap, we set off for a weekend in Dorset, both over the moon. Apart from Mary having one little puke, the journey went well considering she'd never been in a car before. When we carried her into the house we expected her to be overwhelmed by the huge kitchen and hall after the small room she'd been brought up in with her brothers and sisters, but she took everything in her stride. She sniffed around, getting the layout of the place, before we showed her the newspaper for accidents and her water by the back door. After we'd all had supper we settled by the fire. The kitchen was very warm, with an Aga at one end, and our intention was that Mary would sleep alone there at night. So, when the time came, we put the basket by the Aga and said goodnight.

From our bedroom upstairs, we could hear her whimpering. It was unbearable. We couldn't ignore it, whatever the experts tell you to do. Let's just say that one of us was more likely than the other to be told to go downstairs! I tried all the old tricks: a hot water-bottle to simulate her mother's warmth; a ticking clock to imitate her heartbeat; Radio 4 for informative matter. None of them made any difference. We spent the whole night awake, listening to her tiny squeaky howls. Tempting as it was to relent, we remained stern with ourselves, convinced that this stage would pass and a more rugged, respectful cocker would emerge unscarred. After two nights of broken sleep, feeling slightly guilty, we returned to London for her first night in town.

There's a ban on pets, especially dogs, in plenty of apartment blocks. Dogs bring in dirt, bark, aren't always perfectly house-trained and some residents may be frightened of them. Put like that, it's easy to see why some people might not welcome them. I can't now remember whether it was an oversight or an act of denial on our part, but up until that moment we had chosen to ignore all those considerations where our flat was concerned. Besides, who would object to Mary?

We parked in the narrow strip by the side of the building, debating how we were going to get her past Ian, our kindly but strict Scottish porter, who lived in a flat right next to the main front door. There was only one thing for it. I stuffed Mary up my jumper, shielded the bump with various bags and smuggled her into the building. Philippa followed at speed with Mary's basket disguised as an armful of shopping.

When it came to bedtime we remained consistent to the stern training programme we had started in Dorset, leaving her in the kitchen. Equally consistently, she started to whine. Quietly at first, but getting louder by the minute. We couldn't have that. The neighbours mustn't hear. The first of our many dog-owning resolutions wavered. What else could we do but move the basket to my side of the bed – where it's been ever since? Her snoring's the last thing I hear at night, and it's how I know where I am first thing in the morning. When she was little she'd fake going to sleep in her basket; then I'd wake up in the night to find her on my head like warm, hairy headphones, or curled up between our two pillows.

Idiotically, we were convinced that we'd get away with smuggling her in and out of the building under Ian's nose for ever. If he did catch me, I thought, I'd just say she wasn't staying or we'd work something out. Only a few days later, much sooner than I'd bargained for, Ian spotted the wriggling jumper.

'What on earth have you got under there?'

12

I reluctantly revealed our new puppy and made the introductions: 'This is Mary.'

'But pets are against the rules.' Ian was at his sternest. 'If I let you bring her in, then other people will want their own as well.'

'She's no trouble,' I said. 'She's very quiet and won't even be here at weekends. Look at her.'

He stared at her – a golden hand's length with dark wet eyes and ears like bookmarks. How could he resist?

Within moments, infectious denial.

'Well, OK,' he agreed. 'But if anyone sees her, I don't know anything. She'll have to go.'

And so Mary's career of being treated better than the rest of us began.

2

Rusty Bedsprings
by I.P. Knightly

London

*'Those dogs I knew in my childhood
have coloured my attitude to dogs today'*

There have been a lot of dogs in my life, although Mary is the first one with a capital D. My thing about dogs didn't really emerge until I was an adult, but I guess it was always there deep down. Most children love animals and remember a string of them that have passed through their lives in one way or another. I was no exception. There were plenty of pets that crossed my path, almost none of them mine, but many of them making their own small impression on me.

My earliest animal memories are associated with my father, Alec Clunes. I was only eight when he died, so I didn't know him very well. He was the son of music-hall entertainers and an actor himself (I quite like the fact that I'm a third-generation luvvie). But to me he was just my dad, with a voice that I've apparently inherited, and always with a pipe in his mouth. When I was very young we spent all our family holidays in San Telmo, a tiny village on the west coast of Majorca where he'd bought a pigsty that he'd converted into a holiday home. The rest of us amused ourselves as best we could while he built dry stone walls. He was passionate about Majorca and that property. It meant everything to him, to the extent that he left us and went to live there. Shortly afterwards he was diagnosed with lung cancer, being told he had only three days to live. In fact, he lasted long enough to come back to hospital in England where he died three months later.

Without a common language, a dog makes as good a friend as any human. I've still got a faded photograph of me as a child wearing a sombrero and sitting beside one of the local Majorcan collies. Oddly, since I've grown up I've got on less well with foreign dogs. For some reason, they don't get me. I behave in exactly the same way as I would with an unfamiliar English dog, but I never get the same positive response. Maybe it's the diet, the smell or the language. Maybe it's being English. All I know is that they don't engage with me in the way they once seemed to when I was a boy.

At home in England we lived on the outskirts of London, in a two-storey white-rendered Victorian house next to a pub called the Fox and Grapes on the edge of Wimbledon Common – a great place to grow up, with plenty of space and lots of trees. We were allowed out all day long. Everyone knew there was a bit of cottaging going on up by the windmill in those days, but that was largely just smirked about. There was no sense of the predatory that exists today. As soon as I was old enough,

I spent hours out there with my friends, riding bikes, climbing trees, smoking fags.

Apart from those who were walked on the Common daily, there was a small regular cast of unaccompanied dogs who became our playmates. If you could get one to come and hang out with you, you were doing well. The idea of dutifully exercising dogs wasn't on anyone's agenda, but I guess that's what we were doing really. My best friend Jason's family had Katie, a little biscuit-coloured sweetie with maybe some terrier and maybe some corgi in her. Either way, she just liked having her tummy rubbed.

Chubby was another character in our street. He was brindle, with a head like a Staffordshire bull terrier but the body and musculature of a boxer. I don't quite know what was in it for him, but he'd never say no if you asked him to come out. If he had the time, he'd always spend it with us hanging out on the Common. Years later, I discovered his real name was Chappy. Then there was Rusty, a sort of retriever/husky cross. We had a lot of time for Rusty until he ate a neighbour's Yorkie (the dog, not the chocolate bar). As a result of his appetite, they took his knackers away.

Once my friend Paul Hankin and I found two strays, Scruffy and Scamp, and installed them in the empty basement of his block of flats. That was well before we'd got going on the smoking and the kissing (not of each other) down there. We'd take the dogs out and play with them during the day, then return them to the basement at night and give them food and water. After a few days, the police or the lost dog people came along and took them away.

The only time I can remember any trouble with any of the local dogs was when Hushy and Slammie, a pair of Weimaraners who lived in a huge house over the road, attacked me. I had stuffed my pockets with biscuits before going round there to meet a friend, but as I crossed the threshold they went for me. Whether hostile or hungry I didn't know, but they got the biscuits and I got a large purple bite-sized bruise on my thigh.

Those dogs I knew in my childhood have definitely coloured my attitude to dogs today. I love little pointy-nosed terriers like Katie, am always attracted to brindle dogs like Chubby – and not that interested in Weimaraners.

As I grew up, our house was home to a succession of different pets. My father was very keen on cats. His own, Timmy, was a spoilt ginger tom with attitude who ruled our roost. My mother never claimed a pet of her own. She wasn't particularly keen on cohabiting with animals, but heroically put up with all of ours. She always ended up looking after them. Isn't that a mother's lot, after all?

My older sister, Amanda, had a string of pets. She absolutely had to have them and lavished attention on them until boys came along, and one by one the pets took second and then third place. But before that time she had some hamsters whose lives ended in the usual hamster tragedies. They were followed by Tommy, a pretty tabby tom. Or so we thought, until he turned out to be a Thomasina.

Next on Amanda's list of desirable pets was a dog, something I'd never lobbied for. My mother eventually caved in but refused to fork out for one. In an act of selfless heroism, she took Amanda to a local dog rescue centre – and I tagged along. Amanda chose a very pretty, small, predominantly white Jack Russell/whippet cross who sat trembling alone in her pen. She had a sweet, vulnerable little face with a few black spots and a bit of black on one ear. In the interests of punnery she was named Jemima Puddle Dog or Jemima and often 'Mima for short, although years later I somehow ended up calling her Wiggie – I still don't know why. When Amanda and I were at school, Jemima spent a lot of time alone with Mum and clearly thought the world of her. I can only imagine the dysfunctional days they spent together, but I do remember well the look of adoration with which Jemima would gaze up at my mother, her sole walker and feeder.

Among the pets I can remember having myself in those early days were the woodlice I kennelled in airtight containers until my mother punched holes in the lid. They had caramel centres when squashed. The frogspawn I caught was pretty dull, and as soon as the tadpoles turned into frogs they had to be put back in the pond – so all a bit of a disappointment. But we once took my newt on holiday by train in a bowl on my lap. That holiday gave him a taste of a bigger world – Essex, anyway – and he promptly legged it back there when we got home.

When my father died, I was packed off to board at a prep school. The thinking was different then, and there was a worry that if I grew up alone with my mother and sister I would become gay. I was distraught when I arrived there. As a bed-wetter I was put in a room on my own. This was to spare the other boys when the device attached to the plastic incontinence mattress cover that fitted under the nylon sheet hooted when it got wet. Describing the system now, it sounds barbaric, but at the time we were more preoccupied with getting good sparks from the plastic and nylon.

The teachers gave me the job of getting up early (less chance of bed-wetting) to let out the chickens, ducks, geese and turkeys on the school farm, as well as the donkey and the sheep (both out of bounds to everyone else). I liked the idea of being the first person to be up and out – I felt important, with a responsibility of my own. When I'd done that, I came back and made toast for all the rest who were getting out of their dry beds. I liked that, too. It was as if I had something that the others didn't have. After four years of this, and still really good at bed-wetting, I moved up a school to the Royal Russell in Croydon and got to live at home again. Funnily, I was as distraught to leave prep school as I had been when I arrived. However, early mornings remained a feature of my life as I had to get up at 5.45 to catch the 6.30 train to West Croydon in time to get the number 130 bus at 7.15. But at least from then on my bed-wetting was my own business and not a subject for school debate.

After my father's death, Timmy was given an elevated status in the family because of having been his cat. He started having fits that we were alerted to by the thumping of his back leg against the top of the piano, making it ring discordantly round the house. It's a sound I can still hear. Mum was always resistant to taking any of the animals to the vet because of the cost, but because he'd been my father's cat Timmy got taken a little sooner than the others might have done. I didn't know cats got epilepsy, but this is what Timmy was suffering from.

The first dose of the expensive medicine prescribed by the vet stopped the fits but caused a rapid failing of his health. He stopped eating and he stopped washing – the latter being a grave sign in cats. Everything packed up until he fell into a kind of coma. Even Mum was upset. Although Amanda had grown out of her own pets she now became his most dedicated nurse, administering intensive care and coaxing him back to life by giving him drops of beef tea on her finger. Slowly but surely, Timmy began to return to life. From beef tea she got him to take milk off her finger, and then little bits of white fish. Miraculously, he came back to us, but for some reason to do with his circulation the tips of his ears went brown and crispy and then fell off. Notwithstanding, he went into a second kittenhood and carried on as our number one family pet for another six years until he keeled over when he was about eighteen, never having mastered the piano.

As my sister grew up she spent less and less time at home, so it was just Mum and me, and Amanda's pets

Jemima and Tommy. Gradually and informally I became the animals' friend. When I went to bed, I'd have the cat curled up on my pillow, and the dog lying in the crook of my knees. My mother was particularly unkeen on the unhygienic (as she saw it) idea of pets on the bed. She'd tap on the door. 'You haven't got the dog in there, have you, Martin?'

'No!' I'd reply, stroking Jemima. As every child knows, there's something thrilling about the weight of an animal on your bedding. That warmth and the companionship brought Jemima and me together. I remember my daughter Emily when she was four, falling for a visiting friend's Staffordshire bull terrier bitch called Diva. Emily insisted Diva sat on her bed while I read her a bedtime story. Getting the message, Diva didn't reappear downstairs with the grown-ups until Emily fell asleep.

As dogs go, Jemima was quite unexceptional – she didn't do tricks, or anything outstanding or anthropomorphic – but she was very affectionate and grateful for any attention. Once, in the spirit of adventure, I had a mix-up with a bottle of cider that caused me to pass out and vomit at the end of my bed. Panicky about the discovery of both the experiment and its result, I was relieved and impressed when Jemima made the whole ghastly episode disappear in that way that dogs do.

Jemima was always a big defender of the front door. It was the gateway to her territory and she insisted on approving anyone who threatened to cross it. As a naughty boy, I was once caught by the police setting fire to a huge dustbin behind a block of flats. I was ignominiously escorted home by the local bobby, whom we all called 'the sheriff'. We stood on the doorstep, his hand on my collar, as the door opened to reveal my mother with Jemima under her arm like hairy wriggling white bagpipes. Jemima and I eye-balled each other, Mum's hand tight on her collar, the sherriff's hand tight on mine. Mum looked at me aghast before hustling me inside. There may have been some telling off – I can't remember.

By far the most memorable outing Jemima and I shared was when I had a rare day off school and was home alone. Mum wasn't around – she ran an antique shop, and on Mondays and Wednesdays she went off buying. There wasn't much to do – no computer games or daytime TV back then, and everyone else was at school. I was kicking my heels, wondering how I could pass the time. Then I had a brainwave: I'd take Jemima to Harrods.

Jemima had never been on the Tube before, and I had to carry her so her feet didn't get caught in the wooden-slatted carriage floors or on the escalators. Throughout the journey I chatted away to her, making sure she knew where we were and where we were going. We emerged at Knightsbridge and she followed me to Harrods, only for us to discover that dogs weren't admitted unless carried Pekingese-style. Despite never having been to Harrods before, Jemima wasn't at all happy at this arrangement and reverted to her hairy wriggly bagpipe position. We looked at the new TV sets, marvelled at the latest stereos and were shown a fountain pen – by which time Jemima had had enough and we left.

Jemima died when I was sixteen. She'd been suffering from emphysema for about three years. Mum and I (well, Mum) made sure she took her pills every day, but because emphysema's a progressive disease she had to take more and more of them and eventually they ceased to be effective. At the end, she was so out of breath she could hardly walk. My cousin once arrived to find me holding Jemima. 'I'm sure her breathing is easier,' he said encouragingly. 'You're healing her. I'm sure you are.' I wanted it to be true so much that I used to lie on the floor with her back against my chest, breathing in time with her, hoping my good lungs would absorb some of the badness from hers.

Eventually the day we'd been dreading came. Mum did something unheard of and called me at school. I was summoned to the school office to hear, 'We're at the vet's, Martin. He says there's nothing more he can do, and that the best thing for Jemima is to put her down.' Mum knew how upset I was. 'I didn't want to do it without telling you.'

Being at school I couldn't cry, but I still miss Jemima.

We didn't get another dog. I like to think that Mum must have welcomed the end of our pet-owning days with a little sadness, but she probably didn't. No more chasing Jemima down the hall when the doorbell rang or the postman came. No more having to take her for a walk in bad weather or when I was away. No more having to open tins of awful-smelling dog food. No more force-feeding her those emphysema pills. As a typical teenager, my mind swiftly moved on to other things: mopeds, girls – and drama school. I had never been much of a student and emerged from school when I was sixteen with a handful of O-levels and a determination that I should become an actor like my father and his parents. Fortunately the Arts Educational School, then in the City, took students aged sixteen on to their drama course, where I stayed till I was eighteen.

When I left the Arts Ed, I had an agent and a funny face, neither of which secured me immediate employment. By then I was sharing a flat in Putney with a friend called Iain Andrews. To help pay the rent, I got a job washing up in a restaurant in Putney until Iain's brother Clive lied to get me a job at the Great American Disaster, a trendy hamburger joint, where you didn't really need to be able to cook. After that, I got a job scrubbing vegetables in L'Escargot, a smart Soho restaurant.

Iain's mother, Annie, lived in Suffolk where she kept a golden labrador, Puchka, and her two black puppies, Dill and Licorice. Whenever Annie came to London, one or all three of these dogs would stay with us, but most often just Dill. While we were in that flat, someone with whom I'd been at drama school got a job tap-dancing in the Channel Islands (he'd never tapped before in his life) and left his uninsured VW Beetle with us, thinking it would be safe because it didn't have a starter motor. But, without a licence between us, we all learned to bump-start it single-handed, as long as it wasn't facing uphill. I can clearly see the back of Dill's head as he sat in the back seat, waiting for the car to get up enough speed before I rushed round to the driver's door and jumped in. Once we'd got going we sometimes shoved Dill out of the car and made him chase us round Putney Heath or Barnes Common to get some exercise.

At the time Iain was working in the Zanzibar, the coolest bar in Covent Garden, which had brought the whole cocktail ritual to seventies' London. After I'd finished work at L'Escargot, Clive would pick me up in the VW and we'd head off down to the Zanzibar, taking Dill with us. However busy it was, he'd find a corner and lie there asleep until we were ready to leave.

The next dog who really meant something to me was Angus, a slight black-and-tan stray whom friends had found galloping around Highbury Fields in North London. They'd been to the police but no one had reported him missing, so they thought they'd hand him in to a local dogs' home. On their way they dropped in to get some moral support from my then wife and me, who were living near by. I was in the garden sawing a piece of wood when up trotted this strange dog. Our eyes met and that was that.

'Why don't we just keep him?' I asked.

So we did.

We already had Charlie, a Westie, who was my wife's dog, and we weren't particularly looking for another.

But Angus was irresistible. When we went walking on Hampstead Heath or in Highgate Woods, however, his appeal to others was limited. We'd drive there with him not terribly safely on the back seat – his favourite way of travelling was to stick his head out of the driver's window. He ruined countless of my jackets as he regularly tried to claw his way through my right shoulder. I'd have to bat him back as we made our way up the Archway Road. Once off the lead he'd disappear into the thickets, often emerging with a squirrel or baby rabbit that he'd refuse to drop hanging lifeless in his jaws. He would continue the walk, trotting with his head held high, passing horrified parents shielding their children, and black-dressed lesbians muttering, 'Oh God, I can't handle that,' as they hurried away.

Once, in Highgate Woods, he took exception to a police horse and stood in front of it, barking. So well trained was the horse that it didn't flinch, but just bent its head and eye-balled Angus – who stood firm. I kept a respectable distance, nonchalantly calling, 'Come on, Angus!', only too aware I didn't have a licence for him. In those days a dog licence was mandatory. But Angus had no fear of authority.

It wasn't until we were spending Christmas in Mousehole in Cornwall and I saw a foxhound at a Boxing Day meet that I realised that Angus must be a foxhound cross. The slightly domed head was the giveaway. True to his foxhound streak, Angus wasn't much of a people dog and didn't really understand being stroked or sitting close. However, if I was unhappy or upset, which I frequently was back then, he would just rest his chin on my knee and look up at me. If he ever sensed something was wrong – and he always knew – he'd just come and hang out with me.

However sensitive he was, he was always escaping. Once when I was filming *Gone to the Dogs*, a TV drama featuring a three-legged greyhound, a car was coming to take me to work. But a few minutes earlier Angus had run off, and I had to beg the driver to wait. I was worried sick. Sometimes he turned up again, and sometimes we had to go and look for him. This time he turned up – eventually. In the car were Harry Enfield and an actress whom I'd better not name. Without prompting, this actress started spouting off about what awful creatures dogs were. On and on in great detail about why she hated them so much – and the people who owned them. I've never forgotten and never forgiven her. I've loathed her to the core from that moment on. I cannot watch her, cannot appreciate her work. Even if she's giving a brilliant performance, I still think she's rubbish. Thanks to Angus, I realised that I don't like people who don't like dogs.

A few years after coming to live with us, poor old Angus accidentally met his end on an electric railway line while on a walk with my now ex-wife. The news of his death seemed to fit in with all the horrors of a truly rotten period of my life.

3

Betraying Mary

Dorset

'Mary was blissfully ignorant that we had turned our attention to filling the child-sized hole in our marriage.'

I found myself homeless, loveless, dogless and probably gormless, so work became a saviour. *Men Behaving Badly* was at its height and, when I wasn't tied up
shooting it, there were the seemingly endless publicity
junkets and various personal appearances that go along
with being in a very successful series. Around this time,
and through a series of accidents, I'd been asked to
direct *Staggered*, a low-budget feature film that I was
already contracted to appear in. I'd only directed in the
theatre before but I found the enormity of the task
exciting – there was so much to learn and so much to
think about. One of the great things about making a film
with no money is that everyone is there for the best
reasons: egos are put aside and the result is a very pure
collaborative process. The producer of the film was a
tall, elegant young woman with beautiful blue eyes and
an ease about her that made everything we did together a
pleasure. It wasn't very long before I fell head over heels

33

in love with her, a position I'm delighted to say I still find myself in today.

To deal with my homelessness I'd rented a flat that was listed as hard to let. It was in one of those really ugly redbrick seventies blocks on a dual carriageway at the mouth of an underpass. However, once you'd gone up in the lift to the fourth floor and walked as far along the corridor as you could the door opened into a very spacious two-bedroom flat. You could hear no traffic from this side of the building, and the best thing was that every window looked over the river from where you could see the early stages of construction of the Globe Theatre and the South Bank power station that was to become the Tate Modern. The décor was quite scuzzy but eventually I was able to buy it and Philippa and I turned it into our very comfortable first home. Then we got married, and then came Mary.

For three months, life with Mary was bliss. Ian the doorman's caution had been wasted. Her presence didn't spark a revolution of copycat dog owners among the other residents. Mary was just accepted as a popular addition to the household.

Quite pathetically, we stopped going out when Mary was tiny in case she got lonely or upset. When eventually we plucked up courage to leave the flat we asked our friend Hetta to come and keep her company. All she had to do was give Mary love and chicken. Philippa and I went out to eat but we didn't go far, we took a mobile phone and weren't longer than an hour.

Mary behaved so well in our absence that the next time we decided she was old enough to be left on her own. We weren't going out for long, but I set my video camera up on wide lens so that we could see whatever she got up to in our absence. (The one other time I'd used it like this was when I'd set it up to record the visit of the Chinese Prime Minister to the Globe Theatre right across the river from our flat – just in case he was shot.) When we got home, I fast-forwarded through the tape. Another dull hour of video. On the left of the screen was our sofa. On the top of the back cushions perched a small blob – Mary, curled up in her favourite place. She lifted her head once – a bit more watchable than the Chinese Prime Minister, whom I'd recorded over.

Gradually the shade of Mary's coat darkened until it became a russetty gold, although a rather fetching surfer's lick of blonde hair always remained on the top of her head. She grew into her loose puppy skin and her big puppy feet. She was lovely and loving. I can still see her back view flying down the corridor to the flat. Everything we did with her was loaded with 'SP's' Special Privileges. Every weekend we'd take her collar off in the car on the way to the country and put her in 'weekend mufti'. We still say, 'Can you demufti Mary?' when her collar needs to go back on. Sleeping in our bedroom was another SP, as was being allowed on our bed and sitting on the passenger's lap in the front of the car. A prime SP was having a blue pillow in the front of the car that we would plump up and arrange between the passenger and the door to give her a bit of height so she could comfortably see out of the window. Another was going to the office.

Philippa and I wanted to work together so we pooled her talent as a film and TV producer and mine as an actor/director to set up our own production company, Buffalo Pictures. None of the other occupants of our serviced block of Soho offices had set a precedent of bringing a dog in to work, so we did. I don't remember asking anyone if they minded – it didn't occur to us that anyone could possibly object. I began by smuggling her in under my jumper, but as at home it was only a matter of time before my colleagues noticed her presence.

Mary proved to be a great asset to the office. She loved going to work and wandered between my and Philippa's offices on either side of the main reception or snoozed on one of the sofas. She didn't modify her behaviour for the working day, so if there was anything to chew she'd go for it. One of her favourites was any loose electric cable looping around the skirting board. Fortunately we always managed to stop her before anything blew up. She was pleased to see everyone and immediately put people at their ease as she welcomed them, tail wagging, fussing around their ankles. Best of all was when scriptwriters came in to pitch their dreary scripts and she'd either roll on to her back, go to sleep and snore or else rummage through their handbags.

Taking her to work on the set of *Men Behaving Badly* was less successful. Caroline Quentin used to bring Ollie, a tiny, wonderful black and grey and white gay collie cross who looked after himself immaculately and could be relied on not to interfere. He went everywhere with Caroline – as we moved around the rehearsal room, he quietly and discreetly followed her. A bit jealous of Ollie, I wanted to have Mary on the set too. I was sure she'd be no trouble, and I was absolutely wrong. Delighted to be somewhere new, she dashed about, saying hallo to everyone, demanding attention and continually getting in the way. She had no concept that we weren't there just for her. I spent the whole day distracted and ashamed, worried about what she would do next. She was never invited to come again.

The biggest downside about having a dog in a city is having to pick up its poo. If you're going to be a responsible dog owner, it's a must. My pockets were stuffed with plastic bags and I reliably cleaned up after Mary, but how I hated having an audience. Once, as we were walking from St James's Park up to Haymarket, Mary stepped into the gutter to poop. I was standing by poised with the obligatory bag when a woman passer-by stopped. 'Oooh, dog behaving badly,' she trilled. I was tempted to throw it at her. There are a few times when it's not so great being famous.

Mary's first puppy class was held in a church hall in Battersea. It was a madhouse of dogs of every shape and size, some cringing terrified beside their owners while others bounced around, making the most of the opportunity to meet, sniff and greet any dog who showed interest. Mary, however, sat perfectly still under my chair like a piece of porcelain. I had to coax her out for the exercises, all of which she performed pretty perfectly, doing whatever I asked her to do. As I watched and learned, I realised that these classes were for training the owners rather than the dogs themselves.

The Thames Embankment was always one of Mary's favourite places to go walking. The greatest attraction was the joggers who sweated past us, too much of a temptation for Mary. She'd take off after them, yip-yip-yipping at their heels to the enraged shouts of, 'Get your dog off me!' Dog? This was a spaniel puppy, for God's sake. Instead of trying to break the habit, Philippa and I watched her with the pride of parents seeing a child learn a new skill. As the joggers hopped about trying to avoid her, we just stood there beaming.

When she was about three months old, I noticed that Mary was having increasing difficulty in climbing up the sloping side of the flowerbeds on the Embankment. She used to bound to the top, but now she could only reach about halfway before sliding back down. We'd watched her learn to climb these heights, but it seemed that her development was now going in reverse. She also developed a sort of wobbly gait, though not obviously in any pain. I noticed that her kneecaps would slip out to the side. I found I could slide my finger down the length of each femur and pop the kneecaps back into place – but it was never long before they popped out again.

A friend recommended a Dutch vet in Clapham.

'Haf you asked the breeder if she will take the dog back?'

I was shocked she could ask such a question.

'It's a pity you can't get a refund. With any other purchase you would just take it back.'

I nearly took a swing at her.

When the X-rays were ready, the vet looked at them closely before explaining the problem. 'It's as I suspected. She has severe hip dysplasia. If you look here, you can see she also has patellar luxation, which means her knees are poorly defined. So what happens at the hips affects them.'

She went on to explain that hip dysplasia is a condition that more commonly affects the larger breeds, though cockers are prone to it too. Researchers seem to agree that there is some genetic influence, but how much is subject to debate. Looseness in a dog's hip joint results in wear and tear and joint erosion, which in turn leads to arthritis, an incredibly painful condition that radically limits the dog's movement and quality of life. For the symptoms to be visible at Mary's age indicated the severity of the condition: if we didn't have her treated, the vet warned, she might not be able to walk at all by the time she was two. But for the very reason that she was only a puppy and still growing, we would be unlikely to find a vet prepared to treat her. Future bone growth might make redundant any surgery done at this stage, or complicate the condition beyond further help. The obvious implication was that we should have her put down.

Neither Philippa nor I could believe what we were hearing. This was Mary, not some textbook dog. We tried to appear calm, even though we were both really choked up by the prognosis and the decision we would have to make. Of course, there was no question of putting Mary down. I'd seen a couple of dogs in the park who, presumably with some similar affliction, managed to get around on wheels. They weren't elegant or fast but, if the worst came to the worst, I was quite prepared to go down that route. The vet recommended that we took her to Richard Bleckman, a veterinary orthopaedic specialist who had just been chosen as Vet of the Year. His clinic was in a converted public lavatory in Roehampton in South London.

We couldn't have asked for a more considerate vet. Richard seemed to understand exactly why we weren't going to give up on Mary. He was very gung-ho about operating before she was fully grown, and gave us the confidence we needed to agree for him to go ahead. He confirmed that she couldn't afford to wait until she was fully grown; without immediate treatment, she would probably damage herself irreparably. Richard proposed to operate by pinning both hip joints, then cutting open each knee, detaching the kneecap from the tendon, recutting the groove in which the kneecap sits and then replacing the tendon, before sewing her up and tightly bandaging both legs.

But while we waited for the special drill required to operate on bones as fine as Mary's to be delivered to Richard, I had work to do. I had been booked as auctioneer at the Born Free Ball at the Grand Hotel in Brighton, a hotel with a no dogs policy. I rang them.

'Look, we've got a tiny dog that you won't even notice if I bring her along.'

'Sorry, sir. But no dogs are allowed here.'

Time to lay it on with a trowel. 'But she's about to have a major operation. So I'm sure you understand we can't leave her alone. Could we bring her just this once?'

The concierge weakened.

Bigging up the invalid ticket seemed important, so when we arrived we carried her through reception. After a couple of times, the doormen started to greet her: 'Morning, Mary', 'Evening, Mary', 'Nice walk, Mary?'

Mary and I became an indivisible team when I was filming *Saving Grace*, a precursor of *Doc Martin*, in Cornwall. At that time Philippa was pregnant and working in London, so it seemed fairer to take Mary with me. She loved travelling in my VW van, snuggling right up next to me on the bench seat, sharing a pasty on the way. I played the sympathy card again, this time with the St Enodoc Hotel in Rock. She stayed with me the entire time we were filming, living in my trailer when we were shooting and curled up on my pillow when we went to bed. When I wasn't on set I could take her on wonderful

41

short walks along the cliff path or on the beach. I remember some old duffer approaching me as we walked across Daymer Bay and talking to me in rather a pompous way about this and that. To my silent amusement, Mary started following him, walking with almost exactly his gait, as if she was taking the mickey out of him.

Luckily, when Mary had her operation I wasn't far away, filming some rubbish in Wimbledon. When Philippa came to pick me up after work, I was moved to find her sitting in the car in floods of tears. She'd hated dropping off Mary that morning. Our tiny four-month-old puppy had looked up at her with such vulnerable eyes, obviously with no idea what was in store for her that day. We had no real idea either, so Philippa had been shocked and upset to have to pick her up in such a pathetic state. Mary lay immobile on the back seat, still groggy from the anaesthetic, both her hind legs bound in thick white bandages from hip to paw. The vet had said that this was one of the worst cases he'd ever seen.

That night Mary slept by our bed as usual, waking on and off and whimpering until one of us staggered out of bed to give her a painkiller. By the morning she had come round, but was thoroughly puzzled by the strange-smelling white bandages on her back legs that stopped her from walking. We brought food and water to her bed, and had to carry her up to the roof and prop her on her bandaged back legs so that she could relieve herself. We couldn't help being impressed by her quiet tolerance and stoicism. Dogs have no vanity. After a couple of days the pain seemed to lessen and her whimpering stopped.

Her legs were bound for three weeks, and we wouldn't know how successful the operation had been until the bandages came off. We returned to Richard at regular intervals. Everything seemed to be going well until, about three months later, we noticed that she had begun to limp again. A visit to Richard confirmed that Mary's right hip had come adrift.

Recovering from a second operation was much harder because Mary's left leg wasn't strong enough yet to take all her weight, so we had to be careful not to over-exercise her. From that moment on we've always kept a beady eye on her gait in case the same thing happens again. We could take her for short, controlled walks but only on grass, not tarmac; otherwise she had to be carried everywhere. The one positive thing to be said about this stage in her life was that it marked the end of her appetite for joggers. Now when they ran by, she watched them disconsolately, unable to give chase. The negative was that the whole experience marked the end of her open, friendly nature. She remained enthusiastic about anyone whom she had known before the operation, but became less and less happy about meeting anyone new. Instead of jumping up and enjoying the fuss as the old Mary would, she'd come up for a sniff with a wagging tail but as soon as a stranger went to pet her, she'd be out of there.

43

Seeing her go through all that surgery, dealing so stoically with her pain and discomfort, made Mary a particularly special dog to us. We really felt that, because of the gravity and the difficulties of her condition, we owed it to her to give her the best possible passage through life. Our dreams of breeding from her were over. Her Meccano legs couldn't have borne the weight of a litter and, even if they could, hip dysplasia can be hereditary so there was a good chance that she'd pass the condition on. That there wouldn't be any tiny Marys seemed a double tragedy.

Undoubtedly one of the greatest moments in any couple's life is the birth of their first child. When Emily was born, our happiness was elevated to a new level. And as my father-in-law promised, once we left that hospital our lives were never the same again. By this time Mary was one year old and enjoyed the rule of the roost, blissfully ignorant that we had turned our attention to filling the child-sized hole in our marriage. When Philippa went into labour we both went into hospital, where I was allowed to stay for the first couple of days after Emily's birth. All Mary knew was that she was having a lovely holiday with my in-laws, Brian and Lynne, getting spoiled rotten.

We were told that dogs can be jealous when a new baby arrives in the house, but we were confident that if we introduced Mary and Emily in the right way we wouldn't have a problem. After the three of us had settled back home, Brian and Lynne brought Mary

44

back, letting her race down the corridor as soon as the lift
doors opened at our floor. We stood at the front door to
welcome her with Emily in her car-seat on the floor, all
ready for the big meet-and-greet. Mary bounded up to
us, ears flapping, tail wagging, anticipating the huge fuss
she knew we'd make of her.

'Hallo, Mary. Hallo. This is Emily. Look. Here.'

She took a quick sniff at the car-seat as if to say, 'Yep,
it's a baby. So?' And shot past into her domain. Only
when my in-laws left and the baby didn't did it gradually
begin to dawn on her that something was amiss. I now
realise the impact of my own birth on the perfect triangle
that was my sister's relationship with our parents. I can
only say that my sister has borne this intrusion with a lot
more sense and dignity than our pampered pet – but she
did have a pair of perfect and unmodified hips.

As long as Emily was static Mary took little notice of
her, although she must have been aware that our attention was no longer directed solely on her and that we
never went out for a walk without the pushchair. She
was obviously slightly puzzled by the baby bouncer that
hung from a doorway, but made no fuss about it. Emily
offered no in-your-face threat until she began to crawl.
Once she was mobile, there was nothing more interesting to her than Mary's basket where she knew she'd find
the grubbiest and best toys, not to mention the major
part of our attention. At times I thought we must be the
only family where the baby was jealous of the dog. Mary
was never aggressive, but I'd be lying if I said there's

never been a curl of a lip or a growl. Once we were both in the kitchen and Emily was in the living room playing. Suddenly we heard a bark, then a scream. Emily came running in, saying that Mary had bitten her. We scooped her up.

'What happened?'

'Mary was teasing me!' she wailed.

Eight years later, although I know absolutely that Mary loves Emily, she can still sometimes give her the growl. I'm so proud of Emily for not holding that against her. She's learned that it's no more than growling, and still greets Mary and gives her a stroke and a 'Hallo, Mary.' When she comes in to our bedroom in the morning she's always amused to find Mary on top of me, having woken me up about ten minutes earlier.

By 2000, we'd outgrown the flat. We'd looked at a number of small houses in Putney, none of which seemed right. Then one day we were climbing the stairs in a house we felt very positive about when Emily, then a toddler, started laughing. As we laughed back, her laughter became more uncontrollable and Mary started barking. We took this as a sure sign that the house would make a good home for us all, despite its price which was far more than we'd intended to pay. We at last had more space, and Emily and Mary had a London garden.

Whenever the three of us went on holiday, Mary came too. We had to drive because we couldn't take her on a plane – I could never countenance putting her alone in the hold. It was bad enough putting her in a seal cage in a helicopter to the Scillies. She was livid because it stank of seal and she spent the journey furiously cleaning her paws. But thanks to Eurostar, Europe was well within our reach.

In the summer of 2003 we drove through France, staying at different *relais* and *châteaux* on the way to a rented villa in Spain where we were joining my in-laws *en masse*. Everywhere we went there was a lot of Mary fuss. The French were dog-mad and as we went into restaurants greeted us with, '*Ah, le cockeur.*' Whenever we went downstairs for dinner we'd switch on a baby monitor and leave Mary with Emily for extra security – don't try this, folks.

But as soon as we crossed the border into Spain it was, '*Perro? No!*' The Spanish made far more fuss about Emily. But Mary was undaunted. In the car she'd sit up, staring at the scenery rushing past the passenger window.

There's something really funny about seeing your own dog overseas. Watching her at the villa, lazing in the sun or looking out across the Alpujarras, made me happy. We nicknamed her Spanish Mary. On the way home, we discovered a bonus about travelling with a dog. Organising the obligatory visit to the vet within forty-eight hours of boarding for Britain might be an inconvenience, but it means you can sail past the queues at Eurostar by using the Dogs on Board channel.

Three years after moving to Putney, we decided to change the balance of our lives. By then we knew that we wanted to spend more time in Dorset. We loved our life there: the space, the dog walking, the big garden, developing new interests. Our spirits would lift as we passed the model cows on the roof of the Unigate building at the start of the motorway heading south out of London. The deciding factor was Emily reaching primary school age; we realised that we wanted her to grow up and go to school in the West Country. From that point on, the vicarage became our first home and we only returned to the London pad when one or other of us was working there.

Mary went along with the change with good grace. She appeared not to mind spending more time in the country, although whenever her paws hit a London pavement again, I'd swear there's suddenly an extra spring in her step. Then we instituted a third change in her life that she found much harder to accept. We decided it was time for four-year-old Emily to have a dog of her own, a dog that would be a companion for Mary.

So along came Tina Audrey.

4

Back Biting

Dorset

'Mary is a Sophia Loren among dogs, with timeless
looks and good bones – but more regal. By contrast,
Tina's needy like a young actress, demanding as
much reassurance as she can get'

I lay beside the spaniel breeder on the floor of her living room with the tiny eight-week-old orange roan Tina and her blue roan sister between us. Mary was at the other end of the room, looking uncertain. I called her over. She trotted up to us, looked at the puppies and gave them exactly the same treatment she had given Emily on their first meeting. Complete disinterest. She just sat down beside me, threw her ears back and pretended they weren't there.

This was a good sign.

Another search of the Kennel Club website had led us to Jean Ormes, an accredited breeder of spaniels. A sound and knowledgeable woman, she had insisted we brought Mary along to see whether or not she'd welcome the new puppy.

Philippa had always hankered after an orange roan spaniel. They're such pretty dogs, but difficult to come by. I was just glad that we'd chosen to have another bitch

– I've always preferred them to male dogs. They smell much sweeter than the more pungent odour of a dog, especially one who hasn't had his knackers off. And we would get a second chance at having our own litter of puppies.

When we first contacted her, Jean had explained the difference in character between the blue and orange roans. 'Oranges are more vocal and they're harder to pin down,' she said. 'If you have an escapee it will always be an orange. They're very bright and easy to train, but their temperament can sometimes verge on unbalanced. The blue ones are quieter and probably lazier. If you threw a ball for an orange it would go on picking it up till it dropped dead. A blue would pick it up a few times and then hide it under a tree.' We didn't see this as remotely off-putting. If anything this information, together with Jean's impeccable credentials as a breeder, it encouraged us. We decided to wait until one of the rare oranges was available.

Eight months and four litters later, with not an orange among them, we were wavering over taking a blue roan after all; but, having waited so long, we decided to give it one more chance. In the next litter there were two blues, three black-and-tans and three orange roans. The day they were born, overjoyed that the puppies included the orange roan bitch we wanted, Jean called us and emailed us photos. We always look for a lucky spot on our pets and we found this little pup's on her left-hand side – it's now a huge patch. Philippa's mother had had a cocker

52

called Tina when she was a girl, and Emily had set her heart on having her own dog called Tina. I wasn't sure about the name myself, but I was over-ruled. Then we put Audrey on the end – because it added a touch of class and made us smile.

We didn't meet Tina until we could collect her and take her home at eight weeks old. Until then, Jean sent Emily photos of the pups and a big scrapbook packed with pictures of the prize-winning parents and poems she had written about them. At the back she had left several empty pages so that Emily could fill them with her own photos. It's something she'll treasure for the rest of her life.

Jean had been concerned about our already having an older golden spaniel. 'Lots of spayed maiden bitches will be openly aggressive to a puppy straightaway,' she had explained. But Mary had passed the test with flying colours. So now we were driving home with our first dog, her nose a bit out of joint, on Philippa's knee in the front while Emily sat proudly in the back stroking the tiny, cuddly newcomer who dozed on a cushion on her knee.

Jean had advised us to use a crate to give Tina some territory and security of her own while small, as well as preventing her from being a nuisance to Mary. Emily couldn't believe her luck when we put it in her bedroom. She couldn't believe she had her own dog that was her special responsibility, and that night she went to bed as soon as she could. The next morning we found her

53

sound asleep on the floor, half in and half out of the crate, Tina curled up beside her.

The only snag with this arrangement was that, once Tina got her bearings, she always wanted to be wherever Mary was. To Emily's disappointment, we caved in and let Tina sleep in our room, thinking that the two dogs might bond by being together. Both Philippa and I expected Mary's inner mother to emerge soon, but, as hard as Tina tried to make friends with her, Mary wouldn't have it. Mary is a Sophia Loren among dogs, with timeless looks and good bones – but more regal. By contrast, Tina's needy like a young actress, demanding as much reassurance as she can get. When Tina pulled at Mary's ears just as she was getting settled in her basket, or tried to climb in with her, Mary didn't give an inch. She'd respond with that familiar low growl that up till then had been reserved for Emily, and remained withdrawn and unaccommodating. She ignored Tina's yipping at her to play a game, or jumping up at her as she walked through a room. To begin with she saw her off with a growl. When that didn't work, she resorted to giving her a sharp nip.

We thought nothing of this behaviour, thinking it would sort itself out and putting it down to Mary's legs. More often than not the two dogs rubbed along together. On one of our visits to the Cornish Crealy Adventure Park, a place to which we are all devoted, Mary and Tina managed to engineer a joint escape from our van. The first we knew was when we heard on the tannoy,

'Would the owners of two spaniels please come and collect them from the horse race?' We rushed over there to find that they had both somehow got into the enclosure where little mechanical horses moved slowly along a track. Mary had nipped a man as he tried to catch them. He was standing looking furious while she anxiously looked around for us, and Tina raced about like a mad thing. We told them off firmly in public, then popped them back in the car. Despite the looks we got, we actually felt a naughty sense of pride. When they achieve a fame beyond our circle, it just makes us feel big.

About four months later, as she was reaching sexual maturity, Tina was developing into a very attractive but strong and dominant bitch. Now, when she was nipped, she'd nip right back, giving as good as if not better than she got. Given half a chance, she began to give the first nip for no apparent reason and Mary would snap back. We still didn't take their antics particularly seriously, expecting things to settle down. At the beginning they just went for the backs of each other's necks – but it wasn't long before things got worse.

Like all dogs, when they see preparations for a walk – boots, leads, jackets – they get excited. One day, as Mary went to go through the door first, Tina just flew at her, biting at the side of her neck. This time, the aggression escalated into a ferocious fight: a bundle of interlocked, struggling spaniel with snarling, snapping jaws. Blood appeared on Mary's ear. They took no notice of my shouting so I dived in, grabbing at any bit of loose skin I could get hold of, and hauled Tina off. Once we got outside, hostilities ceased, tails wagged and shared sniffing resumed. I dismissed the incident as an over-excited spat, but unfortunately the attacks grew more frequent. The gloves were off.

The wedding of my best friend Caroline Quentin to Sam Farmer was a splendid and joyous affair but one that I missed, having broken down in my unreliable VW camper on the way there with Mary. Luckily Emily, Philippa and Tina were already there, having wisely decided not to come in the van. At the time Sam and Caroline lived at Morebath Manor in Devon, a huge, splendidly Gothic Victorian hunting lodge that looked like a small prep school. They had managed to house almost all the guests with them, and the remainder in nearby pubs and hotels. We, plus dogs when Mary and I eventually arrived, were lucky enough to stay the night in the house.

In the morning, breakfast was a lovely easy event of many sittings, with our dogs and Sam and Caroline's two collies milling around, trying to get lucky with the guests' toast crusts and bacon rinds. Tina and Mary's fighting was still at an early stage and we had little or no formula for dealing with it. To my absolute horror, Tina launched herself at one of the collies, Fenn – who had been so well trained by Sam that one word from him stopped her from fighting back, even though she was only defending herself. Tina, I'm appalled to say, just carried on, trying to push her advantage. Already pretty embarrassed about missing the wedding ceremony, I scooped her up and, feeling the need to be seen to be doing something useful, bit her quite smartly on the back of the neck. And then, God knows why, I sort of shook my head with Tina's scruff still in my mouth. I think I must have thought that it might look knowledgeable and animal-like, as if I was administering the laws of the jungle. Everyone in the kitchen went quiet for a moment, and then carried on with whatever they were doing. I took Tina out of my mouth and popped her back on the floor with an unspoken, 'And let that be a lesson to you!' What a prat.

After a flare-up between our two the dust always settles and Tina approaches Mary, tail wagging. What is it about dogs that makes this happen – one minute fighting to the death, no grudges held the next? At first glance you'd think they were the best of friends. Mary will spend ages cleaning her paws or making sure her stomach is clean. Tina, on the other hand, is always covered in mud and in need of a good brushing. But Mary loves wet fur, so if they've been out in the rain she'll wash Tina's feet and ears, picking and nibbling away until Tina's clean or gets bored and takes a nip at her – whichever happens first. Somebody once said her paw-washing and wet fur addiction has a psychological cause, but I've yet to find exactly what.

Despite their better moments, the fighting continued to get worse and more frequent, reaching a point where

Philippa and I thought that perhaps the only thing was to get rid of Tina. (There was a moment when I thought we had, when she flew out of the car window as we bumped over a sleeping policeman in Richmond Park. She hit the grass verge, rolled over a few times and got up looking dazed. I leaped out, dreading having to break the sad news to Emily. Fortunately no damage had been done.) But finding her another home was the last course of action we wanted to take with such an otherwise sweet-natured animal. We knew Emily would be devastated. Every morning and every afternoon when she gets home from school, Tina's scooped up, squeezed and cuddled.

By now Jean had become a friend of the family. She and Philippa had talked often during our long wait for the right puppy, and had discovered a common love of horses. She was the obvious person to ask for advice. Perhaps if Tina had a litter, Jean thought, she might calm down. If we then kept one of the male puppies Tina would be part of a separate unit, giving and receiving love, and Mary would have a separate life.

We duly sent Tina off to Jean's to be mated. The first stay was short and unsuccessful; the second lasted longer. Jean reported her progress in a letter to Philippa.

. . . I have had Tina for a couple of weeks and I must report she has been a joy. I was concerned when I started to get your news of the problems with her and Mary. I have had no other orange roan I have bred from this bitch behave in an aggressive manner, they are certainly

livelier, more intelligent and a bit more vocal than their blue counterparts. I have not had a litter from Kate since I became aware of the problem but I now feel completely confident in her temperament and happy with her breeding.

She behaves impeccably, is clean, never destroys her bedding. She would sometimes growl if I was cuddling her and Lola jumped up, I just told her no. They have lived together constantly when we are out and have never had a cross word.

. . . We must now find a way forward if you wish to keep Tina and her son. They will be company to each other but ANOTHER SITUATION WITH FIGHTING DOGS MUST BE AVOIDED with three dogs. This may mean making the younger dogs a secure place outside with a facility that is fenced with outside toilet area so that when Mary goes the puppy will be toilet trained and may come indoors. If there is no possible way to arrange this then I would be happy to keep Tina here until circumstances change.

I have observed she has a big appetite and sleeps a lot, so all seems promising as far as her being in pup. I have arranged with a local vet to scan her at 4 weeks 31st May. . . .

. . . In an ideal world you will take Tina and her son home and all will be wonderful, but if that is not possible, if you cannot keep the puppies and Tina in a secure place out of Mary's way, then I urge you not to take her home. I have had people coming to see puppies

*all week and all 16 are sold. I have let Tina and Lola
out with stud dogs and every one has loved Tina. . . .
She deserves to be in a safe loving place. If you decide
that place is not with you then all costs are mine. I pray
you will come to the right decision for all. If after all this
Tina is not pregnant then I think to spay her as soon as
possible. Will this stop fights? Has it stopped Mary from
kicking off? I think it will improve things and you can
only try and if not you must re-home one dog and I will
do anything I can to help. . . .*

Having someone like Jean to give us advice and support
was invaluable, and still is – although, given the way we
felt about both dogs, the last thing we wanted to do in
this instance was take it.

Tina was indeed pregnant, but the pregnancy ended
at six weeks with her involuntarily reabsorbing the
foetuses. Apparently this is something that can happen
if the bitch is stressed or upset, but it may also point to a
more serious problem with her fertility or her ability to
keep the puppies *in utero*. Jean broke the news that this
wasn't going to be the answer after all. Breeding involved too much risk to Tina, and in any case she was
unlikely ever to see her puppies through to full term.
Having been excited by the idea of having our first litter,
we were disappointed. We could only take up Jean's
suggestion of neutering Tina in the hope that it might
calm her down. Although we hadn't yet found a solution, we were all really glad to have her back. We had all

missed her – especially Emily. Tina not being at home was like having part of our jigsaw missing. We couldn't think of rehoming her – but we were determined to find some way to work out the problem.

For Philippa, one of the bonuses of spending more time in Dorset was that it enabled her to take up riding again. While we lived at the vicarage, her horse Bee was kept at livery at some local stables. When one of the stable cats had kittens, Emily and Philippa immediately started campaigning for one. I wasn't entirely against the idea, but any reservations I may have had were in any case swiftly over-ruled. So in came Maisie Anne, a confident, really funny ginger kitten with a bright white throat and belly. I like cats. I'm not one of those dog lovers who see them as the enemy. That said, I wouldn't advise you to lend a cat money.

As soon as Maisie saw Mary and Tina she arched her back, hackles raised, legs stiff with claws out, and hissed at them hard. Mary withdrew and kept her distance, beginning an ongoing process of denial. Maisie still gets into Mary's basket, and Mary is still pretending we don't have a cat. Tina was more intrigued and Maisie soon won her over. They've now reached a position of trust where Tina can drag Maisie around the kitchen floor by the scruff of her neck.

However well Tina got on with Maisie, the fighting between the two dogs continued. So, since mating, spaying and the introduction of a cat hadn't worked, we turned to our vet for help. He recommended a dog psychologist, a young local woman who looked far too smart to be doggy – no elastic-topped trousers or smell of dog. She spent some time with us to see the problem for herself. One of the first questions she asked us was, 'Do your dogs think you're the leader of the pack?'

Yes, we thought they did.

Just at that moment there was a knock at the door and both dogs went barrelling towards it, barking their heads off.

The psychologist looked at us for a moment, then said, 'They *so* don't think you're the leader. . . .' She laughed in our faces.

Apart from witnessing this moment, she didn't see the dogs fight at all that day. We did our best to explain, and we had to confess to Mary's weirdness about the letter-box. If the post arrived when we were out, Mary would chew it up; and if we were in, she'd carefully distribute it to four or five spots around the house – behind the curtains, in her basket, behind the sofa and so on. She was strangely business-like and single-minded about dragging big scripts around the house. Every day we'd have to do a sweep of the ground floor in case something urgent had been hidden.

Mary had become so totally fixated on the letter-box, stressing about the potential arrival of post, that she would sit by the door for hours and hours, just waiting. We'd have to order her off the mat seven or eight times a day. We tried putting a cage over the letter-box to catch the post, but that only seemed to exacerbate the problem and the postman got annoyed because he couldn't always get the letters through. Nor was this behaviour limited to our house. She did the same thing in every house we went to and still does except in our present one – we replaced the letter-box in the front door with a mail-box at the gate.

The psychologist went away to write her report, which she told us would include various instructions that would help us to reassert ourselves as leaders of our pack. The problem lay in our lack of leadership, and we had to treat the two dogs exactly the same. Every time we went through a door, we were to stop either dog from going ahead of us. As pack leaders, we took first place. That did seem to calm things down, since a lot of the aggression often centred on doorways and who went through first. We had to hope that people would wait while we wrestled with getting the dogs into their baskets before we opened the door. At their mealtimes, we had to eat (i.e. palm a bit of biscuit) from each of their bowls, go, 'Mmmmmm, yum,' before giving it to them. That didn't go on for too long! They had to sit and wait until we gave the command for them to eat. At our mealtimes, they had to go into their baskets. That was one thing we were already doing. I can't stand a dog begging. Mary goes automatically without needing to be told.

We did make some headway for a few months and the fighting stopped. But our success meant that we relaxed, and so the whole thing kicked off again.

To complicate matters and territories further, we moved house. Philippa came home from a walk with some friends one day saying she'd seen a dream house that was invisible from the road, surrounded by land and with incredible views. We were very happy in the vicarage, and thought no more of it until we were having lunch with the same people months later; they mentioned that they thought the owner was selling, although she hadn't got round to putting it on the market. One of them called her and arranged for us to have a look.

Set high on a hillside with a view that, on a clear day, extends for sixteen miles down to the sea, the house was a pretty two-storeyed Georgian farmhouse. Beside it stood a two-bedroom cottage and various outbuildings. Outside was a magnificent landscaped garden that gave way to rolling fields. The place was so magical we knew we would never forgive ourselves if we didn't grab the opportunity to buy it before it was put on the market. In the period before we took possession, I used to drive along the road at the top of the land after dropping Emily at school and just gaze at what was about to be our view.

As soon as we moved, in spring 2007, we began to expand our livestock. We started off with rescue chickens – not chickens that rescue you if you're in trouble, but chickens that had been intensively farmed and deserve a better end to their days. Mary has always been fascinated by chickens. She used to stare into a friend's chicken run as if she was watching *Top Gear*. Now she's got her own channel with Muffin, Pirate,

Cookie, Honeysuckle, Sugar Pie, Sheila and the old one, Honor (Honor last legs).

Our next additions were two miniature skewbald Shetland ponies, Hamish and Hector, thirty-two and thirty-five inches high respectively. Why? Because they're really funny. In fact they were such fun that we added two more foals. We wanted a piebald one and a mare that we might breed from, so they were joined by Hamish's brother, Jacob, and Hector's sister, Jemima.

Philippa was the teenager who'd always hankered after a pony as a child but never had one. While we were in the vicarage I'd bought her Prince, a bay ex-racehorse who turned out to have a brain tumour. But not before he'd run away with her. Philippa persevered with him, but in the end we had to give him away. He was the first of a string of horses that we kept in livery.

Emily had learned to ride in Richmond Park on Scoobie Doo, a fat little Shetland from Stag Lodge Stables who has launched a million riding careers. You can see him there every morning with toddlers astride his back, their feet not reaching below the saddle. Tiny, a magical grey with huge eyes, was the first pony of her own. She took Emily up to a really high standard until Emily grew out of her and decided she wanted to start jumping. We were lucky to find a neighbour who wanted Tiny, and in her place we got Saracen, a lovely, unflappable Palomino.

When Philippa decided to go right back to basics we turned to a website specialising in bomb proof horses for the panicked rider. From them we bought Ruby, a hippy grey with a long hairy mane who was so scruffy they wouldn't have her in the livery yard. She turned out to be a little too bombproof, so she went back to the dealer for resale.

Trigger had an unusual talent – a whistling penis. That we could live with, but when he started bucking he had to go too. We were beginning to learn how careful you have to be with horse dealers. They seem to have no qualms about lying their arses off. They deny knowing anything about a bad habit, and then you find other people who recognise the horse saying knowingly, 'Oh, *that* one.'

It was Apache who did the trick. He was sold to us as an Olympic hopeful, although Jean soon put us right on that score. 'An Olympic hopeful would cost more than you could possibly afford.' But he was a beautiful piebald who helped Philippa regain her confidence and got her riding again. With her confidence came a love of dressage, but sadly Apache had a leg injury that meant he wasn't up to it. Finally came Bee, a bay calendar girl who would spook at a dandelion but is otherwise perfect. With our new home, we would be able to stop paying livery fees and have her and Saracen living at home with us.

And then we introduced Arthur Colin, a black labrador puppy, into the mix.

5

Tommy Cooper Is My Labrador

Dorset

'We lost our hearts to him immediately and I knew there could be no going back'

In Port Isaac, where we film *Doc Martin*, there is a daily dog soap opera – not just the dogs of the village, but the many lucky dogs staying there on their holidays too. The locals roam free and meet most mornings on the small beach exposed at low tide beneath the 'Platt'. No fighting here, just happy tail-wagging greetings, and then a race to the water's edge for a ritual splashing and barking session. There must be a saying: 'As happy as a Cornish dog'. We regularly have to stop filming while the beagle – I'm still not sure whose dog he is – saunters through the set. He won't wait and he won't stop, so we do.

During the filming of the third series one of the villagers had a gorgeous black puppy that looked to me like a long-haired black retriever, perhaps with a bit of setter in him. I couldn't take my eyes off him. Over the three and a half months of filming I watched this creature mature from a sweet floppy puppy into a fantastic young dog. His owner trained him meticulously and they went everywhere together. Watching this young dog made me think that if Tina didn't have puppies then perhaps I would one day get a black labrador. Back then it was an idle dream, but once we'd moved and had room for more animals I began to think about the idea more seriously.

The people who we had bought the vicarage from owned Phoebe, a beautiful and kindly black labrador bitch. When Philippa told me that they had a five-week-old litter with one male puppy left, it seemed like serendipity. We went along to meet the litter of seven or eight, all as gorgeous as any other little black bumblebees. First we were shown pictures of the father, and then we met the proud mother, Phoebe. I always love meeting the mothers of litters and getting a chance to make a fuss of them and congratulate them. Her puppies were outside, caged off in the yard. As soon as they saw us they rushed over, jumping up and knocking each other out of the way. Arthur pushed up to us, robust, bouncy and full of character. We lost our hearts to him immediately and I knew there could be no going back. Arthur would be the black son I never had. He would sit tall at my side in my otherwise all-female household. He wouldn't usurp my relationship with Mary – we'd just have a very different one. The owners marked him for us with a blob of pink nail varnish and we went home to wait until he was old enough to join us.

I'd originally wanted to call our new puppy Colin after Colin Grey, my best friend at primary school, whom I've never seen since, but Philippa and Emily completely vetoed this. We eventually reached a compromise that we were all happy with – Arthur, after my grandfather, with Colin as his middle name. When he was eight weeks old the three of us went to collect him at last, taking with us the little collar and lead we'd bought specially for the event. Back in his new home, he was obviously slightly baffled by all the space – very different from the yard that he'd known.

Before he'd had time to adjust, up tapped Mary and Tina to check him out. Arthur immediately lowered himself to the ground in a position of submission, his tail between his legs. He got no change from Mary. She made it quite clear that she wasn't going to take any nonsense from him by growling and refusing to engage with him. Over time, he's learned to soak up her disinterest admirably and sensibly keeps a wide berth. Tina, on the other hand, was initially slightly thrown by this new member of the family, but as soon as she saw that all he wanted to do was play she lit up. They have been inseparable ever since.

When Arthur comes into a room, he bursts round the doorway with an identical energy to Tommy Cooper coming round a stage curtain. He bares his big white teeth in a huge grin just like Mr Cooper. We'd only had spaniels' tiny docked sausage tails in the house for years, and now there's a big, black whippy thing that bangs against tables, chairs and, I'm sorry to say, Mary; not happy. Tina's not bothered, though, because she loves him so much.

I have a feeling that Tina's idea of play is a little warped, since her only play role model when growing up was a growling Mary. Because she had Mary, we didn't think we needed to introduce her to other dogs at puppy classes. She's always been quite a vocal dog and quite wild in her play – but Arthur seems to love that. When he was tiny Tina was very stern with him, but inevitably he's gradually got bigger and, to her astonishment, he's now bigger than her. Instead of, as before, being the underdog submitting to any game Tina wanted to play, Arthur will now take her collar between his teeth and drag her around the room. Sometimes, if he sees her on the lead ready for a walk, he'll bite it and drag her off. She gives in to whatever indignity is forced on her.

Leaving the house for a walk is fraught with difficulty, thanks to Mary and Tina's bids for dominance in the family. But once we've got outside, another fight broken up or avoided, Arthur will charge off ahead before stopping and waiting for Tina. As she gets near, he pounces, snapping at the back or side of her neck. If she's got her wits about her she jumps out of the way, but Arthur's no pushover. If he wants a game he's going to get one, so he tries again, this time bowling her over. Up she gets to scamper off with him, ready to repeat the whole performance. Being bowled off her feet is Mary's least favourite thing, so she keeps a discreet and regal distance behind us, nose to the ground, sniffing out everything good. They all love being taken to the beach and get such joy from being there, Tina and Arthur rolling around in the sea while Mary hangs back doing her own thing, barking and digging in the sand or sniffing about, finding an old rotting squid and rolling on it.

Arthur's an extremely handsome dog with a good stance, a noble head and bright, kind eyes. The Elvis-style curled lip he uses for a greeting is also pulled out when he knows he's been naughty, such as the time when he ate a whole fruit cake. We weren't used to such tall dogs, so had never thought about having to remove food from any surfaces. Given the chance, he'd eat anything and everything until there was nothing left no matter how full he felt. A typical labrador. He's even nicked the eggs laid by our hens. Once, on a walk, he was having a bit of trouble relieving himself. I noticed something pink was hanging out of his bum. Immediately deducing the problem, I stood on the end and pushed him away from me with my other foot so the long pink rubber band he'd eaten emerged with a snap. That's what I call teamwork.

Thinking of his figure, we tried to keep him strictly on dried dog food, but when he realised that Mary and Tina were getting theirs jazzed up with pieces of roast chicken he went on strike and refused to eat until he got the same deal as them. Now, we bung just a little chicken his way and he's easily fooled into thinking that he's got as much as the girls. He also has a penchant for shoes, particularly school shoes, and, like Mary with the post does a lot of shoe delivering round the house. He was always out with the builders who were renovating our house, wagging around, taking them hammers and palette knives, or just picking things up. Retrieving is his gig. Appearing round a corner with something in his mouth, he's Tommy Cooper again with a new magic prop: 'Look at that . . . paintbrush. Ha ha ha.'

Living up on our hill, Arthur wasn't meeting anybody apart from our two strange canine spinsters, some sheep and the builders. At the invitation of a neighbour, I was considering taking him to a shoot. I used to ping away with an air pistol at the squirrels that came to eat the bird food outside our last house. I'd sting them on the arse and they'd run off – I think they enjoyed it as much as I did. But then I scored a lucky hit in an eye or something and killed one. I was so upset that I've never picked the gun up since. I didn't want to shoot anything myself, but thought Arthur would enjoy the running around.

But Arthur wasn't used to the social niceties of life off the farm. He was in mufti all the time, and I hardly ever needed to use a lead with him. On the rare occasions that I tried he was bamboozled by its purpose, rolling over and chewing it in preference to going anywhere. I remembered Dill and Licorice walking down Putney High Street without leads, always at heel. That's what I wanted from Arthur.

Mary's formal training had petered out when her hips went, with the result that she's terrible on the lead. We don't put her on one often, but if we have to, in a public place, she coughs non-stop like an old tramp. Although we hadn't bothered to have Tina trained, I could see that a large dog like Arthur could be a hopeless liability if he wasn't under control. The time had come for puppy socialization classes in the village. I hoped that meeting other dogs would mean he would become as sociable and well-behaved a dog in any circumstances, not just at home.

Rosemary Young, who runs the training classes in Melplash village hall, is an expert dog handler, a Kennel Club obedience judge and an approved instructor of the Academy of Dog Training and Behaviour. Who better to whip us into shape? One Tuesday night, I joined a bunch of eight or so untrained dog owners and their dogs at one end of the hall. Arthur couldn't believe his luck, excited to be among so many new dogs and smells and quite bouncy as a result. He was very taken with a pretty flatcoated retriever called Sophie. He was less sure about Sidney, a gobby terrier who stood up to him. Arthur obviously thought, 'Oh, this is grief, is it? You want a piece of me? OK, then,' and barked back just to show who was boss. But this was the kind of thing he needed to experience so he could be taught how to behave. Some of the dogs were quite wild. One of them, a strong heavy-set black lab called Guinness, was a real handful but was brilliantly handled by the little girl who was training him.

Once the dogs had got used to being together, one by one Rosemary got us to go through the various training techniques: walking on a lead, sit, stay and recall. Arthur proved to be very biddable. I was smugly grateful that he wasn't the one leaping around the room, dragging me behind him.

We weren't very good at doing the homework we were set. Because of where we live, I just did the minimum I needed to go on a walk. But gradually Arthur's got used to the lead and has been very easy to train. I only have to yell, 'Come!' and he'll even give up chasing a sheep or a deer to race back to my side.

Once our builders started removing the floors and ceilings from the main house, we had to move into the very small two-bedroom cottage beside it until the work was finished. With so little space in which to manoeuvre, the fighting between Mary and Tina reached new heights. But nights were manageable. Having become such good friends, Tina and Arthur slept quite happily together in their baskets in the room off the kitchen. Mary, of course, retained her privilege of sleeping upstairs by my side of the bed.

The morning started – as it still does – with a strange pin-down routine. As soon as I gave the word, up she jumped to lie on top of me, with her paws on either side of my face, and gave me a thorough good-morning wash – not unlike John Hurt with an alien stuck to his chops. When she'd finished, Philippa got the treatment. Only then could we persuade her to get down and let us get on with the day.

If we appeared downstairs with Mary Tina would go for her straightaway. To avoid that, we'd smuggle Mary down and shut her in the sitting room before having the morning meet-and-greet with Arthur and Tina next door. When the fuss had died down, I'd sneak out and come back in as if Mary had been downstairs all the time. While Emily distracted Tina, I put Mary into the garden. The minute Tina heard the flap snap she knew Mary was outside and was let out to join her. Then they'd both come in together to find Arthur sitting there smiling, playing with Emily. We all hoped these would be temporary measures until we moved back into the main house, where there would be fewer thresholds to cross and a much larger kitchen.

If we go away, someone has to come in to look after all the livestock. However, we generally take Mary to stay with Philippa's parents. Tina then becomes the dog that Jean wrote to us about. Her attacks are reserved for Mary. She seems to have a dominant aggressive streak that has become exaggerated because we love Mary so much, treating her differently because of her age, her bad legs and her vulnerability, and Tina is jealous of her. Mary may not like Tina, but she would never attack first; she would live quietly alongside her. Mary only fights to defend herself. How could we break what seemed a never-ending cycle?

For four successive summers we had made a series of *Doc Martin*. Both Philippa and I wanted a break, and since starting school Emily hadn't had a summer holiday that wasn't tied to a filming schedule in Cornwall. So we decided to take a year off, during which I would take work that for once fitted in with my family's schedule. An unlooked for opportunity came up early in 2007 while we were filming a *Making of Doc Martin* for Granada Factual. The film-makers saw how much dog action there was around the shoot, from me meeting dogs in the crowd to Mary and Tina visiting the set. Seeing all this gave them the idea for making a two-part documentary about dogs. My initial reaction was that a series about what makes us a nation of dog lovers, with celebrities and their dogs, would be pretty cheesy. I was much more interested in the dogs themselves, the point where humans and dogs meet and why the relationship works so well. At a meeting with the producers I was pleasantly surprised to find that we could make something more all-embracing.

Before we started I swotted up by reading Stephen Budiansky's *The Truth about Dogs*, a brilliant, funny book that taught me a lot. But I was really keen to make my discoveries on camera, so I didn't do much more than that. The questions would therefore be fresh, and the answers fresh to me – a good enough excuse for laziness, I think! The access you get with a camera is always unrivalled. You can go anywhere and talk to anyone, and I knew I would find myself in extraordinary situations with people and dogs I would never otherwise meet.

The more time that I've spent with my dogs, the more I've wanted to know about what makes them and other dogs tick. The more we personalise and humanise our dogs, the more we miss the darker clues to something much older and more interesting. The buried bones, the meals gobbled down at lightning speed, the bizarre obsession with poo all goes back to something ancient and untamed.

I knew they were directly but distantly descended from wolves, but how did we get from the wolf to over four hundred recognised breeds of domestic dog? How has the relationship between man and dog evolved through time? As far as I know, no other two species have a similar interdependency. Did they choose us, or did we choose them? Did early man have the same sort of relationship with his dogs as I have with Mary, Tina and Arthur? And if they didn't, then how and why has the relationship changed as man has messed around with dog genetics to obtain breed characteristics that suit his purposes? Filming *One Man and His Dogs* would give me the perfect opportunity to find out. Perhaps I might even pick up some insights into dogs' behavioural psychology that would help to solve our problem at home, which was getting no better.

6

Good Wolf Hunting
Yellowstone Park, USA

'Genetically speaking, all the dogs that share our
homes are 99.9 per cent wolf'

The fact is that Mary, Tina and Arthur, and every one of the one million two hundred thousand pups said to be born every single day of the year (I don't know who's counting, but that's more puppies than babies), share a near identical genetic imprint with one of the most feared and demonised creatures on the planet – the wolf. Think of it this way: genetically speaking, all the dogs that share our homes, sleep on our sofas, are 99.9 per cent wolf. But there remains an obvious difference between the two species: dogs seem to love humans, while wolves remain notoriously shy. What was it that made the first wolf wimp out of the wild and move in with us? Why did they choose us? Or did we choose them?

Since it's almost impossible to observe the critically endangered Asian wolf, believed to be the direct ancestor of the domestic dog, we travelled to America's Yellowstone Park where we hoped to see the North

American timber wolf. Even finding one of these creatures is not guaranteed. I had been there once before on a day trip from a skiing holiday in Big Sky, Montana, but had only seen the less shy coyote. I was keeping my hopes to a minimum: to see just one wolf in the wild would be enough for me. Visiting the Park in midwinter would offer the best chance. Not only do wolves stand out against snow, but at this time of year they're more active because they're looking for mates and travelling in family packs, covering vast hunting territories. At other seasons they're very well camouflaged and harder to spot. Within this vast snow-covered wilderness, where temperatures were minus twenty degrees Centigrade on the ground, were the beginnings of my journey, my dogs' story and every single canine family tree.

The 2.2 million acres were set aside as a national park in 1872. In the late 1920s, government bounty hunters wiped out the Park's last native wolves as part of a national wolf extermination programme designed to protect ranchers' livestock. After that, the coyote became top dog in Yellowstone. Coyotes are mid-sized cousins of the wolf, having departed from them in evolutionary terms several hundred thousand years ago. They hunt rodents, rabbits and other small prey, whereas wolves go after larger prey, including the coyote. In 1978 Yellowstone was recognised as a World Heritage Site, and in 1995 as a World Heritage Site in Danger. That year, the first wolves were restored to the Park and immediately, with the grizzly bears, became one of the two major attractions. Since the wolf was reintroduced, the coyotes have adapted to their presence by deferring to them and giving them a wide berth.

Doug Smith, a biologist who has worked with wolves for more than twenty-five years, is project leader of the Yellowstone Gray Wolf Restoration Project which has organised the reintroduction of wolves to Yellowstone from Canada. I met Doug at his office in the Yellowstone Center for Resources, a collection of frontier-style buildings including a shop where you could buy beef jerky – there's always one – that made up a few little streets in the middle of nowhere. An impressive, soft-spoken man with a dry sense of humour, Doug was full of his subject without busting out with it, sharing his knowledge in an unassuming way. He was the sort of man who I imagine could light a fire in a blizzard and catch a fish from a frozen lake – all that kind of survival stuff – but without the *macho* that so often goes with it.

About fifteen thousand years ago, our dogs' ancestors came in from the cold and snuggled up to man for comfort. Driving through a brutal Yellowstone winter, it's not hard to see why they didn't go back.

Doug explained that eleven packs co-exist in the Park with roughly ten wolves to a pack, though their numbers can go as high as thirty-seven. His plan was for us to take a route that cut across the territories of five packs, ending up in the Druid Peak pack's territory. Reports were coming through of a kill they had made that morning.

85

My last visit to Yellowstone had been to the other end of the Park, where the landscape had been far less dramatic. But the snow here lay thickly on the trees – even on the thinnest twigs. As we drove through the wilderness, Doug told me something about the wolves. 'Outside the park, wolves do pretty well. But their big Achilles heel is that they clash with people, who don't like them because they occasionally eat their cows and sheep as well as the elk and deer. As a result, the wolf population outside the Park has declined significantly and the density of wolves here in the wild is much higher.' There was no sign of any livestock such as cattle and sheep, but the elk provide plenty of food for the packs.

Doug's theory is that – whether we domesticated the wolf or, as some people say, the wolf domesticated itself to us – through time, wolves changed. 'Just a whisper of a genetic difference means the dogs we have are essentially wolves but modified behaviourally to get on with us. A lot of the qualities wolves have, dogs have in a people-friendly way. Wolf pups are like dog pups because they frolic and greet the adults of the pack, the same way a dog greets his owner when he comes home. Dogs are submissive to humans just like subordinate wolves are submissive to the dominant wolves.'

You can see everything about a dog in a wolf, but a wolf has something else that you won't find in a dog: that wildness, that desire to be always on the move. A genetically pure wolf in captivity will always pace against the fence or the bars. Doug explained that three things make a wolf a wolf: movement, killing and sociability. That last is the thing we've exploited in our artificial selection of them, making a dog from a wolf. 'When I watch wolves in the wild,' Doug said, 'their family fabric is just as strong as human family fabric. In fact, the wolf divorce rate is much lower than the human divorce rate.'

We passed through a beautiful, open, snowy sage-brush plain, the heartland of the Leopold pack, scattered with grazing buffalo and elk, with the occasional coyote skulking, ever-watchful. The wolves have adapted to the existence of the road and, in his fourteen or so years of driving along it, have often crossed in front of Doug's vehicle. Every now and then I thought I spotted a wolf, but it was always either a coyote or a wolf-sized boulder. There's an equal mix of grey and black wolves in Yellowstone, and both their colour patterns blend in well with the rocks. I felt better when Doug admitted, 'I cannot tell you how many times those of us who watch wolves have watched a rock for minutes, waiting for it to move.'

To me, the coyotes looked very similar to wolves, but they're more tolerant of humans. They press the bounds of humanity and panhandle a little more than the wolves will. The wolves tend to stay away from the road, so the coyotes exist in this buffer of safety that the people on the road give them.

The great thing about these sweeping mountain vistas so typical of the Yellowstone landscape is that wolves can be seen from a long distance away through high-powered binoculars or spotting scopes: a gift for scientists collecting data. Before the wolves were reintroduced, Doug and his colleagues expected that they would be as they are in every other part of the world: highly secretive and good at avoiding people. But because they aren't shot or trapped in the Park they're often seen from the road, although they can, if they choose, stay away from people. When designing the research project, Doug hadn't been prepared for that. Most wolf studies in North America are done from the air, but in Yellowstone they've been able to incorporate this advantage of being able to see wolves on the ground.

Some of the wolves wear a radio collar, a sturdy-looking thing with a secure transmitting device attached that allows Doug to tune into a wolf's position. The following day he was due to go on a darting expedition to sedate, capture, collar and then release some wolves. However, the system does have its problems. 'It's difficult to collar wolves. Their winter fur's so thick that, when we put a collar on a wolf, it can slip off in the summer because the wolf sheds so much hair.'

We pulled up near the boundary between the Leopold and Oxbow pack territories and got out of the car, Doug carrying an antenna that looked like an old-fashioned TV aerial. The huge vista opening up to our right was Oxbow territory, where Doug hoped we might pick up on the collared alpha female, the dominant female in that pack. Down below us we could hear the rush of Hell

I was born, Alexander Martin Clunes, in the house I grew up in on the edge of Wimbledon Common on 28th November 1961. Pictured here in the arms of the aptly named Nursey.

With my sister, Amanda, in San Telmo, Majorca on summer holiday. My father had a passion for dry stone walling.

This may have been the last foreign dog who paid me any special attention.

Timmy had an elevated status in our house, being my father's cat.

This is Jemima. My mother was pretty long suffering about our string of pets. I once took Jemima to Harrods to see the fountain pens.

I originally thought this was a photo of my cousin hugging my aunt's dog, Sambo. Then I saw the ear.

Beano days. Hanging out on Wimbledon Common.

My first outing on stage – it was a whodunnit, and
the answer was . . . the cactus.

Gremlin and I on the set of *Doc Martin*. Gremlin, who sadly died during the filming of the third series in June 2007, was greatly loved and we miss him.

With Tina and Philippa, meeting the public and their dogs in Port Isaac on the set of *Doc Martin*.

Roaring Creek, so named because one spring in the early days of Yellowstone a ranger down there was asked, 'What's it like down there?' The snow was melting and the waters were swollen. He shouted back, 'Hell's a-roaring.'

We crunched across the snow to have a good view across the whited-out Yellowstone river valley. The two wolf packs use the river as a boundary between them. Despite being ferociously territorial for part of the year, the Oxbow live right under the nose of the Leopold pack. The Leopolds tolerate them being around, possibly because the Oxbow alpha female is a daughter of their pack.

Within one pack, there's both an alpha female and an alpha male wolf. It's a dual pecking order that rarely crosses over. I asked which of them is ultimately in charge. 'Because historically wolf biologists were male, it was long felt that the alpha male was top dog in the pack. But in Yellowstone, we're finding that it can be either the male or the female, or it can go back and forth within one pack. Who calls the shots is an interesting thing to watch.'

He dialled up the appropriate frequency for wolf number 536 and held the antenna high. I've spent quite a bit of time standing beside people holding those antennae while looking for animals and rarely having much success. All too often the animal has knocked the collar off, the batteries have run out or the antenna doesn't cover a large enough range. From past experience of hissing radios and the endless wait for a reading, my hopes weren't high. So I stood beside Doug, just letting him get on with his biologist thing. Looking across this spectacular but inhospitable landscape, I could imagine a lone wolf, standing on a hilltop somewhere out there, head raised, howling at the moon.

Doug's voice broke into my daydream. 'They love the winter: no bugs, no heat stress.'

'Where do they sleep? Where are their baskets?' Some idiot had to ask.

'Wolves don't need baskets,' he explained patiently. 'They curl up and tuck their nose by their tail. They don't need to be curled up underneath a tree or some place where a human would think was warm and out of the wind.'

'Unlike my dogs at home. They fight for a place in front of the fire.' They wouldn't last five minutes out here, but none the less I was beginning to learn how much they otherwise have in common with their ancestors.

'These wolves don't know what a fire is. They eat their meat raw and they've got thick fur. In my opinion, cold is the wolf's friend. I've never encountered weather too cold for a wolf.'

Having had no success in locating the alpha female, Doug thought we should give up on the Oxbow pack and move on to the Druid Peak pack kill before darkness fell. There was something heroic about the bison we passed en route: ice-covered hulks that lumbered gracelessly into the wind. 'The elk and bison know when the wolves are hunting,' Doug said. 'They don't get too nervous until the wolf's quite close. It's almost as if the elk knows what the wolf's thinking. The chase instinct seems rooted in a wolf's psyche – if it runs, chase it – just as it is with dogs. If the elk and bison don't run, the wolves don't chase. If you're ever in trouble with a wolf, the advice is "Don't run, because you're not going to outrun it."' In the same way, at home, if the sheep are grazing when I take Arthur out into the fields, he takes no notice of them. If they move, I have to stop him chasing them.

We had reached Lamar valley, one of the most beautiful in Yellowstone, but still no sight of a wolf. Above it Druid Peak reigns over the wolf pack's territory. We were in the north-east of the Park, with the Lamar river running on our right and the Soda Butte creek near by. As we turned the next corner, the Asorka mountain range came into view. At its foot in Round Prairie, with luck, the Druid Peak wolves would still be at the kill. Suddenly, a strong smell of rotten eggs drenched the car: a common and not so pleasant feature of the Yellowstone sulphur springs. I watched a coyote steal its way around a group of bison before slinking off through the snow in search of voles or mice.

At a corner in the road, a knot of people wrapped against the elements stood with their spotting scopes trained on something about a quarter of a mile away. In the distance, birds circled in the sky, a sure sign of a kill.

We got out of the car. Without warning, the wolves started howling. The sound reverberated against the cliff face behind them, filling the huge space between us with a chilling lament. I stood rooted to the spot, the hairs on the back of my neck on end. As we listened, Doug explained the reasons wolves howl: to stay in touch with one another when they split up; to identify themselves to other wolves; for group cohesion; for pleasure. In this case he thought that two wolves had separated themselves from the pack and were announcing their approach.

Frustratingly, the camera lens I'd bought specially for the trip wasn't powerful enough to focus on the kill. But the powerful spotting scope Doug hooked up let me see the pack quite clearly, right down to their hairy necks. Two black wolves, the alpha male and his brother, were walking together. To their left was the kill, marked by a couple of elk ribs and an antler sticking up. Surrounding them were the other fourteen members of the pack, seven grey and seven black. Near by, a couple of bison stood quite unthreatened by a yearling pup sitting right in front of them. I recognised aspects of the wolves' behaviour: the cuddling up together; the submissive behaviour when they greeted one another; the wagging tails, the play among the seven pups, pouncing and body-barging, chasing the birds. I was reminded of the day after a party, with the kids running through the trodden-in Hoola Hoops of the elk and the tired-looking adults looking on serenely and proudly: 'That's my boys!'

I would have been excited if I'd only seen one wolf trot out from behind a tree at some point during our drive, but to see all this in the wild gave me real joy. This was wolves doing exactly what you want them to. I felt the same when I saw vultures for the first time. They were fighting inside a zebra carcass – beautiful. There is almost nothing as thrilling as seeing animals in their natural habitat. We had been so lucky to see a kill within a day of being in the Park. We could have been there for two weeks and seen nothing.

The next morning we returned to the kill, arriving before dawn and standing with a group of dedicated wolf watchers, all of us well wrapped up against the falling snow. Doug was picking up a signal which showed that something was happening, but the snow had reduced the visibility. Although the pack would have devoured the elk the wolves were still hanging around, so we waited until the light was good enough to see them. While we waited, shivering in the cold, I chatted to one of the wolf watchers, Laurie Lyman, a retired teacher who for the last ten years had come wolf-spotting almost every day. The scientists can't be present all the time, so people like Laurie volunteer to watch the wolves and record what they see. Doug had a very positive relationship with the watchers, and put the information they gave him to good use. I was astonished that anyone would give up so much of their time to watching wolves – there was something about it that smacked of the hairy train-spotter. Laurie tried to put me right. She had a very emotional attachment to the wolves, unlike other spotters who sometimes approached the hobby as more of a box-ticking exercise. Alpha male – tick. Pregnant female – tick. Four pups – tick. But for Laurie, seeing the wolves obviously meant a great deal more.

'Our goal is to use our scopes as a window into the wolf's world and get a sneak peak at their behaviour and their social interaction,' she told me. 'I believe the wolves are Yellowstone's wild heart and I love to watch the continuing drama. When you look into a wolf's eyes, there's a real intelligence there. They look at you and through you. When they howl as they were doing yester-day it reaches your gut in a way that's hard to explain.'

I hoped she might be able to pinpoint the connections existing between wolves and dogs. The genetic differ-ence is so tiny but, from a human perspective, it's that difference that stops them coming to us and wanting a stroke or to live with us.

'That's true,' agreed Laurie. 'Some people say that when they're puppies, they're puppies, but at about six months old they start to part the ways and that's when you see the wild side of the wolf or the tamer, more dependent side of dogs. I wish more people could see the side of wolves that I've seen, seeing a part of their society and how they operate together,' she went on. 'Hunters or trappers would realise that killing a member of the pack has reverberations. Each wolf contributes to the pack in a different way, whether it's taking care of the pups or hunting or something else. Some of them are loners, but they still have something to contribute. If more humans understood that side of wolves, there would be more acceptance of them sharing the planet with us.'

Some wolf watchers have their favourites, but Laurie tries not to become too attached to any of them. 'Their average lifespan is only four and a half years, and it's as difficult to lose them as it is a pet. If one dies, I feel like I've lost a friend.'

Although we weren't exactly rubbing shoulders with the wolves, having pressed my own eye to the scope I could understand how rewarding it could be to watch them even from a distance. I could also appreciate that if you had the single-minded focus of any of the watchers, the death of a wolf that you'd been following for months or years would have an emotional impact. Wolves inevitably have a relatively short lifespan because of the threats they face in the wild, while our longer-lived dogs spend much of their lives in front of Agas.

The sky had lightened to a uniform pale grey and the wolves were still there. Laurie offered me her scope to watch the pups at play. 'Someone once wrote that the snow is an invitation for wolves to play,' she said. 'And we certainly see a lot of that here.'

I could see that the kill was over. None of the wolves was eating, but they seemed to be in no hurry to move on. I wondered whether they'd be there all day.

'I think so,' Laurie confirmed. 'The adult wolves like to get a place where the pups have somewhere to play and the adults rest up and get ready for the next hunt. It's like watching a playground, with children wandering around looking for things to do. The carcass provides bones and chew toys. I watched two of the pups the other day. One buried a piece of elk pelt. Another watched him, then went over and dug the pelt up. That really upset the first one, who went off and got another piece. They played together with both pieces, then each pup buried their own. The first pup walked away while the second went over and dug both bits up for himself. That probably took half an hour. They sometimes hear rodents under the snow, so you'll see them jump and use their paws to push down on the snow and move the rodent.'

Watching the alpha wolves had shown Laurie that, within the pack, they take a leadership role but not a punitive one. 'The alpha male is a mentor to the pups, playing with them to teach them skills they'll need when they grow up. When hunting, he may help select the animal but he knows his yearlings are strong and fast, so they do a lot of the hunting while he might come in at the end to help with the kill. Once the carcass is there he lets the others eat first, like a general feeding his army.'

Wolves aren't always killing machines. It's interesting how they're out there with bison but it's difficult for them to get one. They put their lives at risk when they hunt, so a six hundred-pound elk is easier to bring down than a fifteen hundred to two thousand-pound bison. If the elk and bison are healthy, the wolves mix with them.

Laurie had even seen one bedded with an elk. 'The elk gets a sense of when they're hungry and when they're hunting, and becomes more alert. But I've also seen the wolves feather through herds of bison and elk, looking for the weak one, the one that's older, slower, ill or lame. The wolves go after the easier prey, not after everything they see.'

So many wrong ideas have been perpetuated about wolves. I don't understand why they have been so vilified in history when they keep such a distance from us. They must have done something to gain such a reputation – or could it have been perpetuated through our ignorance of them? People think that any mushroom that isn't a field mushroom is poisonous. In fact hardly any of them are poisonous – just rubbish to eat. Have wolves suffered from a similar misperception? I couldn't help wondering whether they aren't as dangerous as they're portrayed, but have had an unfair press because they often prey on animals that we herd and farm. On the other hand, perhaps these American timber wolves were homogenised ranch versions compared to the much-demonised wolf of central Europe and the Balkans.

What had surprised me about my experience in Yellowstone was discovering how dog-like the wolves were. When I saw them with the carcass, I couldn't help thinking, 'Mary: chicken.' Seeing them feed, and the pecking order of who gets what and who gets to roll around like an idiot, was completely unexpected. My opinion of wolves had changed. They have an underpublicized playful side and in general seem to be much misunderstood due to the territory clashes with man. The pack mentality and many other aspects of their behaviour make it obvious how closely related they are to dogs.

7

Martin Clunes
Ponces with Wolves

Combe Martin, Devon

'Shaun had crossed a line and was more in tune with his wolves than I could possibly have imagined'

I watched as Shaun Ellis bent forward, hands cupped on either side of his mouth to give him a snout, and took a deep breath in. Straightening up, he breathed out before repeating the process. On the third breath out, he put his head back and gave a long drawn out howl to alert the wolf pack to his presence. Copying his breathing (without the bending and straightening), I let out a higher-pitched squawk of my own that would let them know he had company. We were standing on a small stone terrace, high on a hill, and the sound we made would project across the valley in front of us.

A moment later, from somewhere below, the howls of the pack of wolves reverberated up through the trees. The sound was as I'd heard it in Yellowstone Park, but our surroundings were very different. We were in North Devon, at the Combe Martin Wildlife and Dinosaur Park, where Shaun keeps three packs of timber wolves.

Until the moment I heard the wolves reply to Shaun's

howl, I had been unconvinced about this whole encounter. I was sceptical about wolves kept in cages in England. I was nervous about getting into a cage with them. I knew I was to meet Shaun, a man who'd lived outdoors with these wolves in their cage – how academic, how removed from nature do you want to get? I didn't know what anyone could possibly study in such an artificial environment.

I'm never happy in a zoo, yet here I was in a bizarre built-up environment, with stone paths and oriental bridges, buddhas sitting on the hillside among chilly meerkats and a lone depressive snow leopard. I had been warned that, before meeting the wolves, there were certain dietary requirements: no cheese, no cake, no toothpaste, no soap and no deodorant for twenty-four hours beforehand. I hadn't dared admit that I'd forgotten and eaten a piece of cheese at supper. All this, on top of my preconceptions about a man who put himself in a cage to live with wolves as opposed to living with them in the wild.

When I first saw Shaun I thought there was something definitely wolfish about his unshaven look and his deep-set, piercing eyes. I wasn't sure what I was going to find out about wild animals in this environment. Yet, within the length of that first howl, I had instantly become his pupil. It was immediately obvious that Shaun had crossed a line and was more in tune with his wolves than I could possibly have imagined.

Shaun's howl had been a locating howl, with a final drop note that identified him. Hearing it, the wolves replied, telling him where they were. Once they had quietened down, we listened for the growling and snapping that would indicate they were testing their ranking structure. Now that they had alerted other predators to their whereabouts, they must prepare to defend their territory. His second howl was a 'defensive howl', just slightly different from the first, lower-pitched and intended to discourage other wolves so that our path home would be clear.

We made our way down the path through the trees in which red-ruffed lemurs swung and chattered. We were in no hurry. In the wild we might have to cover six or seven miles before joining them. As we walked, Shaun explained to me how wolves communicate through howling. Their sight may not be up to much, but their hearing is so sensitive that, in good conditions, they can hear rival packs as far as ten miles away. Sometimes a pack will stand in front of a rock face so that the sound bounces off, adding another two miles to its range. Just as I'd seen the wolves do in Yellowstone. Howling is in fact a complex communication system by which the wolves can alert other members of the pack to their location, warn off rival packs, assert their breeding rights, create the impression that the pack is bigger than it is, and communicate a wolf's individual status. Other communication is made through growls, barks, whines, yips and yaps in conjunction with body language.

I didn't know that before. And what he told me about the body language of the wolves was all new to me. I was interested in the barging – Arthur does that – and the leaning. Apparently this is dominant behaviour, testing you to see whether you'll give way. Tina does it on walks when she heads Mary off from the side in a big positioning manoeuvre to show who's boss.

Passing large cages of ring-tailed lemurs and whooping gibbons, we got within sight of the wolf enclosure. Several wolves rushed to the perimeter fence, jumping up in anticipation of Shaun's arrival. A wolf's sense of smell is so highly developed they could pick us up before we were in sight. Their behaviour towards Shaun was the same as if they were greeting one another: lots of tail wagging, licking and sniffing. I stood back, struck by their size and the way their bodies taper from the strong front quarters with large head, intelligent yellow eyes and intense stare to their narrow hips and powerful hindlegs.

Yana, the alpha male and the darkest of the grey wolves, remained aloof, sitting higher up the hill, watching what was going on. Shaun pointed out his distinctive features: his coat pattern that looked as though someone had taken a big black felt pen and coloured in his 'weaponry' or facial mask, the backs of his ears, his hackles and the teardrop-shaped area running down his back.

As a child growing up in Norfolk, Shaun had observed and recorded the behaviour of foxes. As an adult, he studied coyotes in Canada until, after a chance meeting with a Native American biologist at a wolf seminar, he joined a research project studying wolf behaviour in Idaho's Rocky Mountains with the Nez

Percé Native Americans. He worked by day and observed by night, living alongside wolves in the wild for
the first time.

Having returned to the UK, he started working with
Wolf Park Management, an organisation dedicated to the
conservation and preservation of wild and captive wolves
all over the world. The work he has done with captive
wolves in England has taught him in greater detail how
wolves operate in the wild. His knowledge has equipped
him to deal with problem packs as he attempts to restore
the distance between man and wolf, enabling the two
species to co-exist once more. 'Where packs come into
contact with people and where lives are threatened,
there's nobody to act as go-between. We believe that
we could join a wild pack of wolves and, using the same
techniques that we've learned here, instruct them to stay
away from boundaries, farms, ranches, towns and cities.
Wolves kill livestock to get fat into their diet. If we were to
provide that fat for them another way and defend the
livestock, I believe there's hope that these guys could live
in harmony with us once more.'

Four years ago, Shaun hand-reared three wolf cubs
that had been abandoned by their mother – Yana,
Tamaska and Matsi. They were born at the park, their
parents, uncles and aunts being refugees that Shaun had
either rescued or obtained from zoos. When they were
two months old, Shaun moved into an outdoor enclosure with them because there was no adult wolf to give
the impressionable and vulnerable cubs the education

they needed. He was with them twenty-four hours a day for eighteen months, curling up with them to keep warm when he slept and sharing their diet. 'I think of these guys as naturally enhanced. We've given them as much of their wild behaviour as we could, so that we could learn from them and help their cousins in the wild. They taught me far more than I ever taught them. They crossed the species barrier and taught this bungling human who fell into their water and tripped over their logs in the dark to live among them. I don't know whether they see me as human or as wolf. All I do know is that what matters is the position in the pack you hold.'

He confirmed what Doug had told me: wolves withstand sub-zero temperatures by digging a hole in the ground and getting in. They wrap their bushy tail over their mouth, and thus the temperature throughout their body gets regulated. 'There's nothing warmer than having two or three wolves wrapped round you. If you can get to their underside where they release the heat, it's like having your own mobile fires. If you're shivering with cold, they'll come and wrap themselves round you.'

Up till now, nothing would have persuaded me to live in the wild, but I would have liked that. To me, the idea of snuggling up to an animal still goes back to the thrill of having the weight of one on your bed as a child.

Shaun assumed the role of the omega wolf, the peacemaker, in the pack. 'They were once seen as the Cinderella wolf in the pack, because they always look as if they're being mistreated, when in fact they defuse any tension in the pack by attracting attention to themselves in order to restore harmony. As long as you hold on to your position, they respect you. Similarly, a dog may look as if he loves you but in fact his behaviour is a response to the position you hold within the pack. If that position changes, then you'll get a different reaction from the same dog.'

Shaun's view is that dogs usually end up adopting the roles they would have had as a wolf in the wild. The beta wolf will always put himself forward as the expendable one, whereas the alpha wolf will be too aware of his own importance to the pack and so will hang back. Between the mid- and high-ranking wolves is a 'tester' rank. The tester is like a shop steward, who makes sure everyone is doing their job properly. Because the mid-ranks of wolves are followers rather than leaders, they have neutral markings and appear nervous and suspicious. Their job is to create the illusion of there being more wolves than there actually are, which they do by adopting different howls and varying their diet so that their scent markings vary. They usually have the role of early warning system. If your dog is one of these and you live in the city, don't be surprised if it barks round the clock. All it's doing is telling you about anything that moves within a few miles' radius of your house.'

Tamaska, a large black wolf, was jumping up at the netting just as a large dog would. 'We always say wolves are dog-like, but of course the dog got its behaviour from the wolf,' said Shaun. 'The name Tamaska means "mighty" and "kind" and reflects his nature as well as his job in the pack as the beta wolf, the enforcer who disciplines the pack and deflects any danger from the alpha. He's big and bold and comes forward. How many times have you heard people say, "I chose the puppy that came to me first"? Unaware of this pack system, they've actually chosen the dog responsible for discipline in the pack and for safeguarding the alpha parent. That rank of dog would be the ideal candidate for police work, for example. They have the ability to listen to people and then to put themselves between anybody hostile and their handler.'

Based on that explanation, Mary is well and truly an alpha female because she was the one of the litter who hung back when we met her. So Arthur must be the beta male of the pack, while Tina remains a mystery since we didn't get to choose her.

So, in wolf society, every wolf knows its place. They understand and accept social rank. Without this instinct, dogs would never have deferred to humans – which begged the immediate and worrying question: Would these wolves defer to me?

We stepped slowly forwards and, as instructed, I made a paw with my hand and stopped about two inches from the fence. The wolves all trotted up and sniffed at my hand. Tamaska growled at one of the others, ensuring that he was the first one to pick up the information the pack needed from me. As Shaun talked, Tamaska left the fence and returned to the rest of the pack. 'He's taken your smell back to the dominant members. They're going to work out what's going to happen when you go into their territory and whether you present any danger to them.'

I hoped he hadn't picked up on the cheese from last night.

'Yana gets the information from Tamaska without risking himself. If he comes down here and you mean him harm, the entire pack's in danger. When he has the information from Tamaska, he'll make the decision as to what happens next. If he doesn't want you in there, then Tamaska will quickly get rid of you.'

When you're making a television programme there's a rubber band at your back that, deservedly or not, makes you think that someone will whisk you out of a situation that might hit you in the face. So I confidently put my finger through the fence to feel the wolf's coat – the coarse guard hairs that keep them dry and the thick undercoat that keeps them warm. It didn't occur to me that I might be saying goodbye to my finger. By letting them smell us, we were preparing the wolves for our entrance into the pen.

Shaun and his team of helpers separated two of the young wolves, Cheyenne and Tejas, into the pen where I was to meet them. Before I went in Helen, Shaun's partner, briefed me on the meeting. I had to take off my scarf, tuck in my shoe-laces, do up all my buttons and check that my pockets were empty. She took me up to the fence again so that the youngsters could get my scent and greet me there. As the gate opened, Shaun and I walked through purposefully. I wasn't frightened, because I'd seen the crew go through the same procedure – you go first, I'll hold the camera. They hadn't been mauled, but I was aware that there was always a chance that the wolves might take a dislike to me.

On Shaun's advice I stood with my back to the fence so that I couldn't be pushed over, breathing deeply to try to lower my pounding heart rate so the wolves wouldn't sense any fear. That was almost as hard an ask as not being able to eat dairy the day before. My hands were curled into paws so that neither wolf could take a nip at my fingers. I stood looking straight ahead so that when they jumped up at me, their forelegs on my shoulders, I wouldn't get hit on the chin or the nose. Helen and Shaun had warned me that the wolves would try to intimidate me and that my job was to stand up for myself. If they tried to push me, I must push back. 'Own that piece of ground around you, and tell the wolf exactly where you want him to be. They'll test you by rubbing up against you, nibbling you, bumping heads with you. If you don't give way they'll back off, having lost interest until the next time.'

However friendly they seemed, Shaun had warned me not to mistake them for dogs. 'They live by different values to us. They'll show you the utmost respect for going into their enclosure, but you have to reciprocate that. We're in their world and we must come under their rules.'

As soon we were in the pen, the two wolves trotted over and Tejas, the big black one, jumped up. As he pushed against me I found myself instinctively pushing back, matching his pressure. He sniffed my face and nibbled my chin, trying to work out what I'd eaten and therefore where I stood in the hierarchy of things. Chicken? Tosser? Hopeful visitor? At least he didn't growl at me like a foreign dog would have done. Although I had seen the crew go in the pen ahead of me quite safely, standing there with my nose in his mouth was a very different thing.

He turned his attention to my legs, probably smelling my dogs. 'We're not gender-specific to them,' Shaun explained, 'so they don't ask us the questions they would put to a female wolf about speed and direction, the two principal ways the female can dominate the pack. Male wolves answer questions about strength and protective ability.'

Being so close to them, I could sense how powerful they were. They can take down animals that outweigh them by at least one hundred pounds. At the same time, they looked quite cuddly. Crouching down, I stretched out and slowly stroked Tamaska. 'If you put the palm of your hand under the back leg where there's less fur,' said Shaun, 'he'll feel the warmth from you. That's a nice greeting for him. If you were skittish around him that's the sort of behaviour you'd get back from him, but because of the long, slow strokes you're giving him, and because you're calm, he's responding in the same way. Another way of greeting is to lick your lips, drawing their attention to your weaponry. They can see you're not hostile because you're not showing your teeth.'

As soon as I tried this, Tejas came forward and started licking my tightly shut mouth. I'd been warned about getting some unwanted tongue action . . . I've worked with actresses who are similar (and one actor!). Once he was satisfied I went through the same process with Cheyenne, the only female in the pack. The females are usually smaller, faster and therefore often the hunters in the pack. Once both Tejas and Cheyenne had accepted me in their territory, Shaun and I could move across to a rock where we could sit while he talked more about the wolves and the distinction between them and domestic dogs. What intrigued me was the importance of the pack structure. I had thought that the pack broke down into alpha and beta wolves and the rest. That was it. I had no idea there were so many distinct roles within a pack. In fact, every wolf knows its place. They understand and accept social rank. Without this instinct, dogs would never have deferred to humans. Shaun explained why.

'Imagine if I sent you into the wild with only a pack of wolves to protect you and your family. You would have to develop a family structure to look after you all. You'd need someone to make decisions about the environment; someone to protect you; someone to alert you to danger; someone to hunt. If you didn't have animals to fulfil those places quickly, then you'd have to breed them, recruit them from other packs or take in one of the lone wolves operating in the area.'

What I'd need would be someone to give me instructions. I respond to clear instructions in the home – that's why I married a producer.

Tejas came over to greet me again, this time standing behind me, higher on the rock. 'That's where he feels you're most vulnerable. Most people would react by pushing him away, and that would show him how strong they are. The easiest way to get a wolf's respect is to unbalance him by gently pulling one of his legs. Then his attention will be focussed on that rather than on you. If the other adults in the pack felt he was getting the better of them through his strength they'd simply drag a front or back leg away, showing who's the master of his balance.

'These guys have been taught that they don't need to fear man. Their cousins in the wild know that if they come near us there's a good chance they'll be killed, so they run away. Not having that flight instinct is a contributing factor in the development of dogs from wolves. I believe that if we bred on from these wolves, we wouldn't go through very many generations before starting to get the floppy ears, softer fur and different colour pigmentation of a domestic dog.'

I'd read that in 1959 a Russian geneticist began an experiment to breed a population of tame silver foxes. After eight to ten generations the colour of their coats changed, their ears began to flop and their tails curled up. After fifteen to twenty generations their tails and legs were shorter than those of the first generation. By selecting the tamest animals in the programme, he speeded up a process that had taken thousands of years of natural selection to produce dogs from wolves.

I wanted to know whether Shaun felt that genetics were responsible for the difference between wolf and dog. He thought not. 'It's the environment they're brought up in and the society they keep that shapes an awful lot of their behaviour. You can see exactly why early man was tempted to take a wolf from the wild. Man could harness the animals' skills, using their ability to hunt and move faster than us as well as their acute sense of smell that can help as an early warning system.' And let's not forget the companionship, the warmth and the good feeling you get from being around them.

Watching Cheyenne licking Shaun's face, I desperately wanted her to nuzzle me in the same way, clicking her teeth against mine, rubbing her head up against me. She seemed to be communicating with him. I always push my face into a friendly domestic dog's face and let them greet me in the same way. I lowered myself so I was sitting on the ground and licked my lips – and over she came to give me the same treatment. Arthur behaves in exactly the same way with Biro, an older lab that belongs to one of our builders, nibbling at the side of his mouth as if he was a pup hoping for some food. When Cheyenne was nuzzling me, I felt great. But although I was told that this was the wolves' way of receiving the information they needed from me, I wasn't getting anything from them.

Shaun went on to tell me how at an early age the wolves learn various calming techniques that can be effectively used with dogs too. For example, lying on the side, exposing the underbelly or adopting the suckling posture of the mother will calm a dog or a wolf very quickly. (And some actresses, too.) This harks back to the time when they were suckling in the wild, pressed close and safe to the mother's chest (not the actresses). To reassure her offspring of their safety, the mother would breathe in and out so that they would connect with the rise and fall of her chest. If, when older, they're not close enough to feel the movement of the chest, they can still hear the sound that goes with it. So if a dog looks at you and exhales heavily, and you exhale back, you're telling each other to calm down, that everything's safe. These are techniques Shaun has learned from the wolves and practised successfully on his own dogs. I've never tried any of them. Perhaps I should. The only successful calming technique I use is to rub between a dog's front legs – works like a charm every time.

Something else we can usefully adapt from life in the wild is the wolves' alarm call when they make an 'uff-uff' sound or a half-hearted bark. 'If you are teaching a dog not to touch something,' explained Shaun, 'copying that sound would be more effective than a shout he doesn't understand – because the dog would automatically con- nect to a sound taught him by his mother as a warning.'

That afternoon, we watched the wolves feed. The pack maintains its hierarchy through diet, so it's essential that the wolves are fed in the right way. If they ate beef joints, all the wolves would eventually smell the same; the rank distinctions would then be lost and the pack structure would break down. The right diet is a complete carcass so that Yana and Cheyenne, the alpha pair, can get the high-status food and the lower-ranking wolves the lower-status food; in this way, they will all smell right. It may look like a free-for-all, but in fact the feeding routine defines the pack hierarchy.

Shaun entered the pen to squat by a stag's carcass, holding it so that the wolves wouldn't move it to a more sheltered place. A few deep breaths to centre himself and he was ready. The wolves thundered through the gate to rip the carcass apart, growling and snapping as each one defended his or her own area of food. The wolves ate around the brains, heart and liver that were reserved for Yana, the alpha male, who stood apart from the rest of the pack while they fed. Tamaska, the beta male, ate the good-quality 'movement meat', while the lowest-ranking ate the stomach contents.

Shaun was right there with them, licking and snarling. When a fight flared up, his job as omega wolf was to placate – so he flung himself head-first between the two wolves in question, positioning himself below the higher-ranking one. I'd have stopped laughing if he'd been bitten, but I could see he was so confident with them that I couldn't help myself. Perhaps I was shocked by the unexpected way he shoved himself so close to those snapping jaws. His swift intervention worked. The wolves quietened down every time.

This behaviour reminded me of the way Tina attacks Mary and then, moments after being pulled apart, goes up to her with her tail wagging, the previous few minutes apparently forgotten. Shaun explained a common misconception. 'I think the perception we have that a dog is being friendly when it wags its tail isn't true really. Every time a dog raises, lowers, wags or circles its tail is a form of communication, but not necessarily that the animal's friendly. He may be agitated or showing aggression.'

While in the enclosure, Shaun remained alert to the movement of every wolf in it. Hand-reared they may have been, but these animals are not domesticated and aggression can flare unexpectedly. 'The omega role is central because it calms a hostile situation and is therefore crucial to the structure of the pack itself. At the moment that's my position in the pack, but if I had to leave for some reason one of the guys might step into my shoes. If that happened, it might be dangerous for me to return to the pack.'

Cheyenne, the alpha female, looked as if she was adopting the same sort of role as Shaun, but he assured me that her behaviour was her way of charming food from the boys. 'She knows she hasn't got the weight of the big males, so if she goes up against them they're going to get the better of her very quickly. She uses her brainpower rather than brute strength, and succeeds more times than she fails.'

Watching Shaun with his wolves and hearing him talk was impressive. He was clearly passionate about the wolves and about putting his knowledge of them to practical use. From the outside they look so like dogs, exhibiting so much of the same behaviour – except they are dogs to the power of ten. My dogs can't smell, hear or hunt like wolves. They certainly don't look like wolves and they wouldn't last five seconds in a fight with a wolf. Yet, visiting Shaun's wolves had made me see more clearly how the domestic dog had descended from them. I had also been given an insight into pack behaviour that is still relevant to today's domestic dog.

By the end of a day with Shaun, my preconceptions had been completely overturned. My initial scepticism had been replaced by huge respect for a man who had lived with these animals for eighteen months and has a deep understanding of wolves, dogs and pack behaviour. I wouldn't live with wolves and share their food myself, but I live with cocker spaniels and give them my chicken so I've got my own version. I had imagined that a formal distance would be kept between the pack and me but instead, from the moment I put a finger through the fence and stroked them, I realised that they were looking for some sort of social interaction with me. I've been around lots of animals, but it wasn't like being around anything other than a dog. They were doing what my dogs would do – only more so.

8

Dingoes in Danger
Fraser Island, Australia

'Lots of people will tell you that the only good dingo's a dead dingo'

Mary suffered two drastic hip operations in her first year. After that, we felt it was our duty to make sure the rest of her passage through life was as comfortable as possible—and so began her career of being treated better than the rest.

Mary is a Sophia Loren among dogs, only more regal.

Hitchcock Mary

Mary with my wife Philippa outside our farmhouse in Dorset.

We really wanted an orange roan for our next dog. And, in the third litter, there she was. Tina Audrey, third from right.

Tina and trophy bride (on the left).

Emily, my daughter, is devoted to Tina.

My first coyote.

The frozen beauty of Yellowstone National Park was a dramatic place
to witness my first wolf kill.

This landscape reminded me of a Dali painting.

An heroic bison.

I wasn't sure what to expect meeting wolves in captivity. I'm never happy in a zoo.

Shaun Ellis, who has hand reared these wolves, lived with them in their enclosure for eighteen months. There is something almost wolfish about his look.

The wolves were so dog-like in many ways, but it was clear that they viewed Shaun as one of them.

It's all about trust.

Dingoes on Fraser Island National Park,
Australia, at sunrise.

As the single-prop light aircraft circled over Fraser Island, just off the Queensland coast of Australia, I looked down over the dense rainforest, interrupted only by tea-coloured and clear blue lakes. I'd come all this way to take a look at the dingo, the dog believed to be the closest we have in appearance to the proto-dog, the first domestic descendant of the wolf.

I'd left home secure in the knowledge that Mary and Tina were going through a quiet patch. Whether it was the dog psychologist or us, or a combination, I didn't know, but the fights seemed to be breaking out less often. I was relieved that things were going well when the time came to leave Philippa and Emily. As for the destination, I was looking forward to seeing for myself what dogs looked like before we started messing around with them and developing different breeds for different purposes.

Fraser Island is the world's largest sand island, a World Heritage Site where domestic dogs have been banned since the early 1990s so that the dingoes here remain one of the purest strains in eastern Australia. Domestic dogs would once have accompanied the men who worked for the logging and sand-mining companies, but all that changed when the island became World Heritage listed. However the dingo has an international reputation for aggression, particularly since the notorious Chamberlain case when one snatched a baby. On mainland Australia feelings towards dingoes are divided – pest or pet? I hoped to find out the truth. But with over six hundred square miles of rainforest and only between one and two hundred dingoes left, they were going to be hard to spot.

On my first morning there I met Colin Lawton, the chief conservation officer, who had agreed to drive me round the island in search of dingoes in the wild. With his enviable protruding ears we were quite a match. I liked him for those (he'll never starve!) and for his dry Australian wit. We set out before dawn, snaking very slowly across the island on narrow sand tracks where, in the headlights, we could make out dingo paw prints. We drove to Seventy-Five Mile Beach, a knife-edge of white sand on the eastern, surf side of the island that doubles as its main highway and airstrip. We broke through the dunes on to the sand just as dawn was breaking, lemon-yellow light streaking across the sky. Sunrise and sunset are the most likely times to spot a dingo on the beach. Sensibly, they take shelter during the hottest part of the day. 'We don't recommend people walk on the beach by themselves because, if they met some dingoes, they might get themselves into a bit of trouble by doing the wrong thing,' Colin warned.

There, right in front of us, two beautiful, lithe dingoes were racing along the edge of the water, silhouetted against the rising sun. Oblivious to us, they chased each other through the surf until, suddenly aware of our presence, they stopped for a moment to take us in. Standing stock still, ears pricked, tails hanging low, they stared until they had taken in all they needed to know about us, then took off again with a bound. They were obviously having a ball, playing in the surf, enjoying themselves in exactly the same way as Arthur and Tina do on the beach. I found it hard to imagine them living up to their reputation for aggressiveness. These dingoes were so confident, so much at home in the landscape, that I watched transfixed until they disappeared over the dunes into the rainforest behind. They seemed to share the pleasure in just running that I see in my dogs at home.

I knew that, if I met one, my immediate instinct would be to greet it like an ordinary dog with a pat or a stroke, but Colin warned me off the idea. 'People get too close, and children especially wave their arms or run about. That triggers a reaction in the dingo to chase you and test you a bit more. They test a response from you to see what you're likely to do. If you give the wrong response, then things can escalate into aggression.'

I was reminded about Shaun's advice concerning the wolves. Never underestimate a wild animal. What we think is two dingoes playing is in fact one animal establishing his dominance over another. Depending on the dog's mood, a human reaction could trigger a violent confrontation. 'It can be very frightening, especially if there's a pack of dingoes. They'll circle round you, and while the one in front's keeping you busy the others are trying to sneak in behind you.'

Like the wolves, each pack of dingoes establishes a hierarchy that divides its members into dominant and subordinate animals. This is a system based on aggression and is used against the pack next door. It's important for each one to know where it is in the system. When a dog gets old and weak, the younger dogs will eventually see it off or kill it if it isn't killed by a rival pack. Each pack of dingoes scent marks its own territory. However, their territories do overlap and one pack can move through another's territory, but this is usually done at particular times of day so that the packs avoid each other as much as possible.

As we drove the sun was rising, burning through the early morning mist. I asked Colin how the dingoes arrived in Australia in the first place.

'They were brought over by Asian seafarers about four or five thousand years ago as both companion and hunting dogs. At that time, the main predator in Australia was the thylacine, or Tasmanian tiger. They were a similar-sized animal to the dingo and an apex predator, which meant that they weren't preyed on by other species. Some think that the dingoes put an end to that and helped with their extinction.

'Aboriginal people would certainly have helped with the distribution of the dingo throughout Australia. To-day, dingoes are in every habitat from desert to island to rainforest country. They're adaptive animals that can survive pretty much anywhere. The Aboriginals would have used them as companion animals and for assis-tance with hunting, as many Aboriginal communities still do today. Dingoes are a very special animal, and appear in their mythology and dream stories.'

Colin went on to explain a bit more about how dingoes fit into the story of dogs. 'There are thought to be two diverging paths in their evolution. Those from western Asia seem to have been subjected to much more selective breeding pressure to produce traits that people wanted at that time. They're more the precursor to the domestic dogs you get today. The suggestion is that the dogs from eastern Asia were left to their own devices, so that the general consensus of the scientific community is that these are pretty much the same as primitive dogs. The pack system and their range of coat colours are both close to what they were five thousand years ago. The fact that dingoes throughout Australia and South-east Asia behave the same way, despite the diverse habitats, suggests that they all come from the same original stock.'

Even though domestic dogs have been banned on the island for the past ten years, a little evidence of some hybridisation, or cross-breeding, in the dingoes here is still evident. Modern domestic dogs have a shorter, smaller snout than the dingo, smaller molars and short-er, more slender canine teeth, as well as shorter ears.

Colin was keeping a keen eye out for dingo tracks in the sand. All he'd seen so far were those that he thought must already have been there before the tide came in. Over the radio a fellow ranger reported seeing some tracks heading into the bush, and we decided to go up there to take a look. I leaned out of the window with my camera at the ready. In the continuing absence of any dingoes, I amused myself by photographing the local birds. Then at last I saw one sitting stock still in the sand. On closer examination it turned out to be a large piece of driftwood doing an Oscar-winning performance that had me fooled.

The number of dingoes living on the island is hard to establish exactly. However, Colin estimated that there are twenty-five packs with five or six dingoes to a pack. The three or four summer months see the highest population, when there are pups on the ground.

A minority of people on the island mistakenly still think that they need to feed the dingoes. As a result, the animals sneak around town or the campsites, scavenging scraps that are deliberately put out for them. The rangers worry about this because the dingoes tend to become reliant on handouts and gradually lose their hunting instincts. Eventually they become demanding and confrontational – a situation that no one wants. In

2001, a dingo killed a child on the island. I was told that the boy had been running away and the animal had caught him with an unlucky bite on the leg. Since then, a more intensive dingo management programme has been in place. 'Our two main aims are the conservation of the species and the safety of the general public,' Colin explained. 'Basically, it's about keeping the dingoes and people apart so that you're not getting those negative interactions or that close contact that teaches the animals bad habits that lead to confrontations. So we talk to people about their food security, and we have enforcement powers so we can book campers for not putting their food away. Instead of the old open dumps we consolidate the rubbish by putting the bins behind fences. We discourage campers from cleaning fish close to their tents. We've also put up fences around some of the resorts and camping areas to keep a buffer zone between the animals and the people.'

There are four dedicated staff on the island to deal with the dingoes while others spend time educating the public. Scientists carry out research here on the behaviour and ecology of the dingoes. Colin and his colleagues hope that the Fraser Island dingoes will become the purest population on the eastern seaboard of Australia and possibly even Australia-wide. They really are a critical population in terms of dingo conservation.

In mainland Australia dingoes are frequently regarded as a pest and there are regular culling programmes to reduce their numbers. Colin confirmed that strong

emotions were involved, making the dingo's conservation something of a battle. 'In Queensland, there are two
separate legislative obligations. On protected areas of
national park, the dingoes are considered a native species and therefore need to be protected. But once you get
off those protected areas, they're considered a pest
species. There's an all-out war against the dingo in
pastoral areas, particularly sheep country. Pastoralists
have been trying to annihilate dingoes for the last couple
of hundred years with major baiting and trapping pro-
grammes. Lots of people will tell you that the only good
dingo's a dead dingo.

'A lot of the grazing industry has helped the dingo
population as it has set up more water points, more food.
Most states in Australia have conflicting legislation when
it comes to the dingo because there's confusion as to
where the dingo sits in the big picture. Some people
question whether the dingo should even be considered a
native species.'

But for a place like Fraser Island, the dingo is an
important part of the tourist industry and brings considerable economic benefits. The dingo packs are a
thriving attraction which, along with the bird and marine
life, brings plenty of visitors to the island.

Some people say there's not enough food for them
here and that's why they hunt for the odd piece of ham
or saveloy, but Colin assured me that the dingo is
naturally a very lean animal and the population self-
regulates to whatever is available to them. On the island

there are a couple of species of bandicoot, small mammals that look a bit like a rat, that are the dingoes' most popular prey followed closely by four or five other native rodents. They'll also take down the small wallabies that live on the island, and eat reptiles, especially the big skinks, and some plant material. Sometimes they hunt singly or in pairs, but if the prey is something like a larger kangaroo they'll switch their hunting tactics and work as a pack.

During the breeding season, in April and May, they spend much more time in the pack, bonding to make it stronger and for greater success when hunting. At other times of year the associations in the pack are much looser, so the animals only meet up every few days. It's Fraser Island's bad luck that the time of greatest dingo activity coincides with Easter and the school holidays, one of the most popular tourist seasons. Then again, the whelping season in August and September coincides with one of the main fishing seasons, when the tailor fish and the mullet run.

By this time we'd reached Yidney Rocks, a modern beachfront apartment complex not far from Happy Valley, one of the two major east coast settlements. I'd almost given up on the dingoes and had got taken up with the bird life although, frustratingly, I recognised nothing except the screeching seagulls. Colin pointed out crested terns, a willie wagtail and some lapwings.

We still hoped that a local pack of dingoes with pups, that had been regularly seen on the beach by the resort where we were staying, on the west side of the island, might turn up in the afternoon. 'It's dingo heaven around here,' Colin admitted. Nice restaurant smells, food and rubbish. We've put a fence around the resort on Kingfisher Bay to keep the dingoes out, but this is a fairly regular haunt of theirs. It's a harder life for the dingoes on this side of the island, with fewer prey resources. We try and hunt 'em out of the high visitation areas, trying to instil a bit of wariness back into them.'

Swifts were darting across the sky, and pelicans bobbed on the sea as we walked along the sand.

'Look! Look!' Excited, Colin was pointing towards the dunes. 'There's a dingo pup.'

But the pup had disappeared behind a fallen tree trunk. We walked towards the top of the beach in the hope that he would reappear. Just as I was losing hope, there he was, standing on the edge of the scrub. His black and tan coat was in good condition, the outline of his ribs just showing through. His snout shaded from tan to a black nose, while his bright brown eyes looked warily about him. He was a beautiful dog, with pricked ears and bushy tail. For me, this was another endorphin-releasing meeting. A small group of people had gathered to stare at this beach celebrity, but kept a respectful distance.

'Have a look at his feet,' Colin urged me. 'People talk as if all dingoes looked the same, but if you look closely you'll see they have different white socks and often a little white tail tip. I'd say this one's three to four months old – just weaned. So he's probably just started to look for solid food within the last few weeks. Mum'll be around somewhere.'

Mum was in feet keeping her distance, but she must have known that her pup would be safe here. There's no negative reinforcement for the animals on Fraser Island, so as long as humans didn't get in the way he wasn't going to get in much trouble.

Back at the resort, I had a call from Philippa. I was looking forward to telling her and Emily about the dingoes, and was keen to hear how everything was at home too. But instead of giving me the usual reassurances that everything was fine, Philippa was in floods of tears. The tension between Mary and Tina had escalated since I'd left and they'd been fighting two or three times a day. This day had been the worst yet, with five fights. She was at the end of her tether as she told me what happencd.

'I was in the paddock with the minis, breaking the ice on the water trough. On my way back to the house, I was on my mobile when I heard a fight going on ahead of me. I dropped the phone and ran to the dogs. Arthur was in there as well, although he looked as if he hadn't a clue what was going on. I was trying to separate them, but it was so vicious that I couldn't get them apart. There were teeth everywhere. I was screaming at them to stop, but that only made it worse. As I pulled Tina and Mary apart by the scruff of the neck, one of them bit me. It was such a frenzy that I haven't a clue which it was, but the teeth went right through my jeans into my thigh. Blood and a big gouge in my leg. It's agony.'

I knew only too well how difficult it was to separate two scrapping dogs if there was only one of you. We had never imagined that the fighting could get this serious, and certainly not that anyone would get hurt.

'This is the worst fight there's been,' she went on. 'I can't stand it any more. We've got to do something. I've got to get Tina out of the house.' What worried her most was the thought of Emily getting involved. If there was a fight and she crouched down by them with her face at their level, it could be disastrous.

I did my best to calm Philippa down and to persuade her to give Tina one more chance. 'Ring some kennels and try to get her in there until I get back,' I suggested, although I knew that the week before Christmas would be the worst time of year to try to find anywhere. I wanted to delay making any irrevocable decisions until we had time to talk it over properly. We both knew Emily would be devastated to lose Tina. By the time we'd finished talking, we'd agreed that once Philippa had been to hospital for a tetanus injection she would find Tina somewhere temporary to stay. She agreed, but I could hear in her voice that she wasn't happy. There was nothing more I could do till I got home except rack my brains for a solution.

The following morning, very early, Colin and I had one last crack. We were up again at 3a.m. and bouncing along the sandy tracks with the same sense of anticipation, watching out for the clear dingo tracks in the sand. As we drove on to the beach I spotted a beautiful tan-coloured bitch swaggering purposefully around some houses, obviously on the scavenge. She looked at us, then came alongside the car so that I could see her markings quite clearly: a white snout, underbelly, inner legs and under-tail. Like the dingoes I'd already seen, she looked very canny: she knew quite well what she was doing and where she was going. As I watched her she watched me, keeping her distance before she disappeared into the scrub.

Although we'd spent hours looking for the dingoes and only seen a few, these few made the waiting worthwhile. I'd expected something much clubbier in the head – more of an Ernest Borgnine of a dog – and couldn't get over how slender and athletic they were and what fine features they had. To think that all the other breeds of dog in the world have resulted from man manipulating their genetics. The only thing that, for me, slightly diminished the thrill of the occasion was that the dingo on Fraser Island has become such a tourist attraction: dingo tea-towels, dingo postcards, dingo key rings. At the same time they have to be kept away from the tourists, and vice versa. What Colin said was obviously true: for hundreds of people, seeing a dingo is the highlight of their trip – just as it was for me.

9

Dinky, the Singing Dingo
Alice Springs, Australia

*'Accompanying a dingo on the piano, has to
be one of the best moments of my life'*

The only thing that made me somewhat wary of Dinky, who lay stretched out asleep in the sun, was the heavy chain that secured him to one of the verandah chairs. He seemed blissfully unaware of my arrival. Perhaps a lazy eye opened, then shut. Otherwise, he didn't move a muscle. This was Dinky the Singing Dingo, the star attraction at Stuart's Well Roadhouse, about sixty miles south of Alice Springs.

We had driven for an hour and a half into the red centre of Australia without a break in the litter by the side of the road – mainly tinnies and fag packets tossed out of car windows, but I saw bits of cars and any old rubbish as well. That aside, it still feels as if you're in the middle of nowhere. Only as we pulled up did I realise I'd been there before. Seven years earlier, when Neil Morrissey and I had made *Men Down Under*, a documentary about the essence of the Australian male, we'd come to ride camels on the farm next door. We'd raced them round the dunes, and when we'd finished filming we agreed to ride them back with Noel, the owner. That was great – no cameras, the pressure was off and he was giving us camel-riding tips. He tried to get me to do 'round the world' on the camel's back, where you swing your legs over to sit facing each direction, one after another. I really didn't want to, but he insisted. 'Come on, mate. Swing yer leg over. Go on. That's right' – and I fell off. My best tip for riding a camel? Get a horse.

The sun had been blazing down as I walked from the petrol station to the typical Australian roadhouse: single-storeyed with a green corrugated iron roof. Skirting round its verandah, past the sign to reception, I'd turned the corner to find Dinky's owner, Jim Cotterill, out the back, straining the swimming pool, his dingo in the shade near by. Jim was a grey-haired man in his sixties with a full beard. The roadhouse policy regarding Dinky is, 'No touching, no problems.' As Jim pointed out, if everyone on the bus tours that stop here were to pat or stroke Dinky, he might get a bit peeved by the end of the day. 'On the occasion when people have been ahead of me and they put their hand out before I've had time to say, 'Don't!' he has been known to growl. If they persist, he's been known to snap just in front of the hand, but he's never bitten, never grabbed. Just given a warning.'

Having seen the dingoes of Fraser Island running free in their natural habitat, encouraged to keep separate from man, it was fascinating to meet a dingo who went against everything I had learned so far. Dinky was domesticated, talented and loved. The chain rather suited his delinquent look. After watching a Stacey Keach film in which he played a lorry driver with a dingo (played by some sort of cattle dog) I had always expected the dingo to look more like Dinky, or like the rustler in *Wallace & Gromit's Close Shave*.

The first thing Jim did was introduce us. Sitting on a chair beside him, I stayed quite still while Dinky stood and sniffed my legs. At seven and a half years old Dinky, a typical inland dingo with a tan wiry coat, had a slightly grizzled snout, wise brown eyes and pricked ears. The only sign that he's different from any other dingo was his heavy studded collar. On Jim's strict instructions I didn't put my hand out and looked over his head, careful not to intimidate him by staring directly into his eyes – avoiding all the things I would normally do on meeting a domesticated dog. After he'd had a good sniff I got a lick on the knee, and I was then allowed to stroke him behind his ears while Jim held him and told me his background.

When the European settlers arrived in Australia they brought farm animals with them. By then the dingo was the main predator in Australia, a territorial pack animal which kills for the sake of killing. 'Once they start, they get into a frenzy and keep on killing,' Jim told me. 'But they don't eat what they kill – just take a couple of choice pieces.' Inevitably, because farmers suffer serious financial losses when their livestock is killed, they trap, shoot or, most commonly, poison dingoes. 'When my father brought us here from England in 1952 the farmers used strychnine, but now they use 1080. You'll see warning signs on fences and gates, because the killing is controlled by the conservation people to bring the dingo population down to a manageable level.' I hadn't realised that, unlike domestic dogs which can have two litters a year of as many as ten puppies each time, dingoes only have one litter of five or six pups. Once domestic dogs start breeding with dingoes, these crosses can outbreed the dingo and have the same character traits.

A nearby farmer was conducting a dingo-poisoning programme when a station hand came across a litter of puppies. 'Dingoes often go to the back of caves to give birth or they dig deep burrows, like rabbits, and have their pups underground. This station hand could hear them whimpering and crying. He guessed their parents had been killed, that they were hungry and thirsty, and decided to save them. He made a wire cage and set it over the entrance of the burrow to catch them when they emerged. He gave me this one.'

Dinky looked like a pretty placid creature to me. 'Oh, he's wonderful,' enthused Jim. 'He lies around all day, absolutely quiet. He has his own chair to sleep on in my house, but if something happens outside he'll come into the bedroom and push my foot with his nose. If I ignore him, he'll come round the side of the bed and punch me in the back with his nose. Then, when I'm awake, he glides across the floor on the balls of his feet so you don't even hear his toenails on the timber floor, and jumps up on to a bench or a cupboard. He sits looking out of the window, without making a sound.'

I was so pleased to see that Jim was as soppy as hell about him. Remembering all that Colin had told me about the hierarchy of the dingo pack, I wondered whether an obvious hierarchy existed with Dinky, Jim and the other members of his family. 'Yes,' he was quite definite. 'I have to be the alpha male. My first wife and I had three sons. When Dinky was a puppy, they weren't terribly tolerant of him. They were never physically violent or nasty, just the verbal, "Go on, you mongrel. Go away." He remembers that, and he ignores them. I'm married to my second wife now, and when our two daughters were young they would cuddle him, feed him and make a fuss of him. They are his sisters now. They're away at uni most of the year, but whenever they come home it's a delight to see his reaction. He runs home and puts his legs round them and cuddles them.'

After everything I'd heard about a dingo's aggressive behaviour, I was astonished by what I was hearing. Nevertheless Dinky's genetic coding meant that the aggression native to the species was still there under his skin. Jim had a small animal enclosure where he kept kangaroos, ducks and emus. He wouldn't let Dinky roam around outside on his own in case he got in and killed them, but at home things were quite different.

'My wife has a small dog she calls Little Miss Scruffy. She's got such wiry hair and a bit of a beard that I thought she must be a gremlin when I first saw her. Now

I think she must be a miniature Irish wolfhound. When I took Dinky home, I thought, "That's it, the little creature's dead." On the contrary – she ran over to Dinky for a bit of play and that was it. They jump and play around the house: Dinky goes over the furniture and Little Miss Scruffy goes underneath. He opens his mouth and Scruffy puts her head right inside. There's never been any aggression between them.' I asked if Dinky had any other dog friends. 'There's a couple out the back here, a border collie and a blue heather cross, that we use as deterrents to stop people jumping the fences. Dinky goes out the back and runs with them. But he's the boss, and after two or three minutes the game's over and he comes back, scratching to be let in at the back door.' But Dinky is, of course, best known for his singing talent. Once his gifts had become known Australia-wide, Donna, a hearing dingo from Sydney, and her owner, John Hogan, visited Alice Springs, prompting the headline in the local rag, 'Donna the hearing dingo will listen to Dinky the singing dingo.' Another dingo owner from Perth met the four of them at Alice Springs railway station with his own animal, Lindy.

Dinky's singing career began when one of Jim's daughters took piano lessons. 'Any time the girls were at home playing, he'd just get up on the stool alongside 'em, throw his head back and give us some vocal rendition. We called it singing, avoiding using the 'h—' word. He started singing when other people played, and then found he could climb up on to the keyboard and sing there. "Hey, I can make these noises myself." '

He also uses singing as a form of communication. If left in a room by himself, Dinky gets anxious. But Jim can't let him roam free – he has no choice if he doesn't want carnage in the animal enclosure or for Dinky to be mistaken for a wild dingo and get shot walking down the road. So if he wants Jim's attention, he hops up on to the piano and sings, 'Hello! Where are you? Come and get me. I'm lonely and bored.' I think that's by Lionel Richie.

Not everyone is impressed by Dinky's talent. One woman who was part of a coach party heard him singing and 'She thought it was the "h—" word,' Jim protested. 'By the time she came round the back, I'd brought him outside and put him on his chain. He was jumping around, wanting to get back in. Well, she heard the singing and saw the jumping and said, "That dingo's stressed. He needs to be put back into the wild. This is unnatural. He hates it. The sound of the piano was hurting his ears." Now, if he didn't like the piano, he wouldn't go anywhere near it.'

What I'd found here with Dinky was a domesticated wild animal that likes to be treated like any domestic dog. The only time he gets stressed is when he's left outside and wants to get back inside to be with his pack of roadhouse staff or family. He even likes to be with the visitors, provided they don't try and touch him. He's introduced to new staff in exactly the same way as he was introduced to me. He does his thing, has a sniff and then, three or four days later, he'll turn his back and point his bum at them. That's an invitation to scratch the top of his hips and signifies his trust. I'm the same.

Jim and I had talked enough. It was time to hear Dinky do his thing. We roused him from where he was happily lying and went through the large sunlit restaurant to the 'piano room'. At one side stood an upright piano against Dinky's 'wall of fame', which was covered with newspaper cuttings, letter, photographs and cartoons from all over the world, including a receipt for a charity donation. Jim proudly told me that Dinky's playing has raised fifteen thousand Australian dollars for charity in the last two years, primarily for the Flying Doctor service. On the piano stood a statuette of a dingo standing with its forelegs on a piano, its head thrown back in song. There was plenty of Dinky-nalia to be bought too. Again, here's a dingo as a visitor attraction – but this time the dingo apparently got a lot out of it too. I bought Emily a stuffed Dinky. Not much of a substitute for Tina, if it came to it.

When the twentieth anniversary edition of Trivial Pursuit came out, the game's manufacturer, Hasbro, offered one thousand Australian dollars for a new question to mark the occasion. 'My wife heard this on the radio and mentioned it to one of our daughters, who was home for the summer holidays. She composed and sent off the question: "What is the name of the internationally acclaimed piano-playing, singing dingo that lives in central Australia, and where does he live?" The first I knew was when I had a call from Sydney about four months later. "Hallo. I'm the marketing manager of Hasbro. We'd like you to fly Dinky to Sydney for press interviews." What press interviews? I had no idea what she was talking about!'

His wife put Jim in the picture, but he was still unhappy about putting Dinky in a dog box on a plane. 'I said, "He'll go ballistic. At the very least he'll eat his way out of the dog box, and more than likely he'll dig a hole in the floor of the plane. This could cause some problems. No, I'm afraid I can't send him to Sydney."'

Three days later, the marketing manager arrived in Alice Springs with a film crew who spent three and a half hours filming Dinky singing with different people. 'That's when she said, "Oh, by the way, he's not a finalist, he's the winner. I'll send you a cheque for the thousand dollars."' Jim laughed. 'That's when I thought I should have taken the whole litter! Of course, I sent the money to my daughter, but that was the turning point for Dinky. The day after the press release about the new Trivial Pursuit question went out, we had the BBC from London, Birmingham, Wales and the Canadian Broadcasting Corporation ringing for live interviews.'

At Jim's invitation I sat at the piano, beside a chair for Dinky, and struck up a few notes of chopsticks – the only tune that Emily's taught me. As I rapped out the first bars, he hopped on to the chair and then on to the piano keys. He stood quite still, raised his head and sang.

It did sound a little like the 'h—' word to me, but professional pianists had told Jim that Dinky actually changes harmonics to suit the variation in key. The higher notes bring out his inner Sinatra, whereas he doesn't respond to the lower registers. Dinky's stance suggested to me that he wanted to dominate the piano, but he made no move to stop me playing as he concentrated on reaching the end of the song. Accompanying a dingo on the piano has to be one of the best moments of my life.

When I called home that night, it was to discover that things were no better. Philippa hadn't had the heart to leave Tina at a kennels after all. 'It was freezing cold and I couldn't put her in an outside kennel and walk away. I just couldn't.' In desperation, she had phoned Jean. Jean had always felt that Mary might never accept Tina and that, if necessary, she would take Tina back. Philippa had reached the point when she had to take her up on her offer. True to her word, Jean agreed to take Tina and find her a new home, even though it was so close to Christmas.

The only way to get Tina to Jean's was to find a cab. Only one of the local firms was willing to take her, once they'd checked their insurance and Philippa had bought them a dog seatbelt. When Philippa had broken the news to Emily that Tina's cab had been ordered, she was distraught, as predicted, and had shut herself in her bedroom, screaming that she'd never forgive us if we sent Tina away. When she'd calmed down, all she'd said was, 'My heart is breaking.'

I felt completely helpless, stuck on the other side of the world. Emily came on the line, and I asked her how she felt about Tina going.

'I know it's got to happen, but my heart's going to break,' she sobbed. 'I love Tina and I don't want her to go away.'

'But we can't live like this, sweetheart. We can't have her biting, can we?'

She agreed we couldn't. The three of us tried to work out some other solution, but as far as Philippa and I could see we'd tried everything. Although we thought we understood the psychology of what was going on as they fought for the position of top dog, we'd failed to find a way to change the dynamics. Just when relations between the dogs seemed to be getting better, we'd relax and the fights would kick off again.

There was no question of Mary going. We'd been through too much with her to be able to send her away. Perhaps she was giving out signals that we were unaware of but that provoked Tina. Whatever was going on, she had never initiated a fight, just responded to Tina's attacks. Having Arthur as a companion for Tina, however successful in some ways, hadn't drawn the heat away from Mary, who was simply reacting to Tina's aggression. Nothing would stop Tina pouncing on Mary when she was asleep in her basket, or on the sofa or under the table. As a result, Mary crept nervously around the house, unsure where she should be. That was gutting to see. Yet, on her own, Tina was the most delightful dog and Emily absolutely adored her. The decision to get rid of her couldn't be taken lightly.

IO

Domestic (Dis)harmony

Alice Springs, Australia

'It's not a dog, it's a dingo. What's his name?
Dingo – that's it'

A long time ago I remember hearing a theory that dogs and men first came together via the dogs' interest in and use for our refuse. This appetite can extend far beyond the obvious – I won't be too graphic, but there are dog-keeping tribes whose babies don't need nappies. I can't say that this rubbish theory convinces me one hundred per cent, but they do love leftovers and they are fascinated by the bin, aren't they?

To illustrate this theory for the TV show we'd lured an eminent veterinarian, Associate Professor Paul McGreevy from the University of Sydney, where he heads the faculty of veterinary science. Paul is a really nice sensible bloke with an enthusiasm for his subject that knows no bounds, his speciality being dog and horse behaviour and welfare. To make the point we'd gone to film his interview on a rubbish tip on the outskirts of Alice Springs. Research had revealed that the feral dogs that fed and scavenged here were very elusive, and so to keep the camera happy a couple of people had been hired to bring along some feral-looking dogs and have them rustle through the rubbish in the background. However, the minute the dogs got out of their owners' cars they took a cursory stroll over the smelly rubbish (the temperature was over twenty Centigrade) and then went back and sat underneath the vehicles. The next plan was to secrete food around the dump and in the back of shot. Unfortunately this didn't do the trick either, as the dogs had just been fed. Luckily, Paul McGreevy is so smart he can make a point without illustrations.

'One theory is that man played an active role in the domestication process. Another theory, and it's not exclusive, is that dogs domesticated themselves,' Paul began. 'They were attracted by our rubbish that included faeces, food scraps and rotting carcasses.' So when early man chucked a chicken drumstick over his shoulder, there was a wolf to catch it. Gradually the two species came closer and closer together.

'We then capitalised on dogs as resources for guarding and keeping the place clean. The first pups selected from those early proto-dogs would have been the produce of the least fearful parents. So the first step in the domestication process was accomplishcd when those parent dogs overcame their fear because of their need for food.'

The obvious difference between the two species is that, generally speaking, wolves are fearful of us and dogs aren't. But Paul seemed to be saying that there was a species that existed between wolf and dog – presumably the proto-dog. Paul confirmed this. 'There is a missing link in a sense. I like to think of the proto-dog being wolf-shaped but having certain characteristics that allowed it to come closer to us than most wolves would.

'We were both beneficiaries in this process. Dogs don't have to hunt any longer. They don't have to worry about competing with other dogs or being killed by them. We provide them with warmth, shelter and companionship. At the same time, we've used them more than we have any other species. They've been used in warfare, for food, for haulage, guarding, hunting, transport. We've used dogs for every possible use a domestic animal can be put to. We've even used their fur as fibre. So they are the most useful of the domestic pets and we owe them a great deal.'

Our two evolutionary paths have therefore been adjacent. The litters of pups that the early humans raided and chose from would have been the ones closest to human settlements. They would have been the pups of the bitches that had fed the most on our waste and were therefore more fertile than the underfed bitches. Dogs were drawn to our resources and we were drawn to the closest pups. 'It's called co-evolution and it's still going on,' he added. 'But I think that we, as guardians of the dog, need to look at the bigger picture when it comes to keeping dogs healthy in the future.'

In Paul's view, domestication isn't a process that's complete. As he sees it, dogs are still passing and failing the domestication tests we give them. 'You can think of dogs in a pound as having failed a domestication test of sorts. They may have run away from home because they were scared by fireworks or a thunderstorm or because they've bitten someone out of fear.' The Cornwall Crealey Adventure Park loomed large in my mind as I remembered the man whom Mary had bitten furiously waiting for us to come and get her. Despite failing that domestication test, at least she had escaped the pound.

Paul was concerned with the criteria that we should be using when breeding dogs these days. 'When we think about how to move forward we should be selecting dogs that are good companions, but unfortunately we don't have good tests for companionship. The only temperament test a dog has to pass in the show ring is not biting the judge.'

I was struck by how true that was. There is no test for best temperament or best dog with children, or most obedient dog. This is a criticism that the Kennel Club is beginning to address by introducing new classes such as Most Handsome Crossbreed Dog, Prettiest Crossbreed Bitch, Child's Best Friend and Golden Oldie Crossbreed in their Scruffts competitions.

What always makes me laugh is the idea I read about in *The History of Dogs*, that when a dog barks he's really only saying, 'Hey. Hey. Hey.' I know I shouldn't anthropomorphise my dogs, but I was delighted to hear from Paul that research is being done into the dog's laugh. In America, zoologists have been doing work on dog vocalisation. Research shows that a particular rhythm of breathy exhalation that most of us would dismiss as panting can trigger playfulness in other dogs. Running and playing with another dog is obviously an extremely rewarding thing for dogs to do. I'm delighted. Why can't we say that they enjoy something when they obviously do? With all my dogs I can tell the difference between running as a way of getting from A to B and running with joy. For instance, they launch into a run for joy. Tina's a great one for running with a springing, joyful step. My childhood dog Jemima used to tuck her bum under her like a whippet and run: that was running for joy. Arthur does it a little bit, too. It's not merely a means of transportation but a dance of freedom.

This talk about good behaviour in dogs made me think about what was going on at home. Would Tina have eaten her final meal, made her last requests? That night, Philippa rang me to say that Jean had called her back and suggested that, instead of rushing to rehome Tina, she and Emily might put up the crate that had come with her and place Tina in it in another room. 'Never leave the two dogs in the same room together,' was Jean's advice. 'That'll get you through till Martin gets home. Sending Tina away is a big thing to do. Once she's gone, she's gone. I know how upset you all are. So before you send Tina back to me, why don't you take a look at some DVDs I've got?'

The DVDs had arrived the next day. Tina's cab had been cancelled, and in galloped Cesar Millan to the rescue. Jean had always said she didn't rate any of the dog gurus, but this one was different. Millan, celebrated in the USA, explains his work quite simply: 'I rehabilitate dogs. I train people.' The DVDs were from his *National Geographic* series *The Dog Whisperer*, in which he successfully dealt with dogs exhibiting aggressive or dominant behaviour. His methods involve giving dogs 'rules, boundaries and limitations' and establishing a pack order. Philippa was shown a way of dealing with Tina at last. Nothing we had done so far had alleviated the problem, but when she followed Millan's technique of forcibly putting Tina on to her back as soon as she showed any aggression it seemed to pacify her.

'I have to grab Tina and hold her down with a very relaxed arm till she calms down, Philippa explain. She growls and goes mad for thirty seconds. Then Mary comes and sniffs her, I let go, and they both stand there and wag their tails at each other. It's completely bizarre.'

She was also experimenting with Millan's techniques of 'energy blocking' by getting between Mary and Tina to block a bad look, the sign of an imminent fight, and distracting them. Although that demanded constant vigilance when they were all in the same room, she seemed to be getting a good result there too.

I was relieved that Tina had a stay of execution and that Jean was helping Philippa find ways to cope with the situation. Having stared in the face the possibility of

Tina being rehomed, we didn't want to go there again. But before I could go home and try these dog-whispering skills out for myself, I had one more dingo to see.

Another of the reasons for coming to the red centre of Australia was that I had read that dingoes played an important role in Aboriginal Dreamtime, the belief system that underlies their origins and culture. Each tribe has its own Dreamtime, although many tribal beliefs, secrets and superstitions overlap. However, most of the Aboriginal lore is kept secret from all but the initiated.

Uluru or Ayer's Rock is Australia's most famous landmark, but it also has great cultural resonance in Aboriginal mythology. Similarly, other physical features in the landscape have their own mythical associations. Flying in a helicopter over the terracotta-coloured McDonnell Range, I had a perfect view of Mount Gillen: scrubby sandstone mountain that dropped sheer away on one side. At its foot lay the modern industrialised urban sprawl of Alice Springs, its white roofs glinting in the sun. The white fellas make a big song and dance about how important Mount Gillen is to the dingo and to local Aboriginal people from the Arrernte tradition, even though they have no idea exactly why. The story has it that the mountain was carved out by a dingo defending the land against intruders. But its spiritual significance is apparently so great that none of the Aboriginal people would tell me anything about it: any questions on the subject were effortlessly and elegantly diverted. We were told that whoever broke the silence would die, or at the least be stabbed in the leg, as would the person to whom they were speaking. Suffice to say that Mount Gillen is unique in its importance to the relationship between Aboriginal man and dingoes. The only rather inadequate analogy I could think of was that it was something like a cathedral to dogs.

When Neil and I filmed *Men Down Under* we studiously avoided the question of Aboriginal people because, when we were doing our research, so many nervous white men had warned us to stay well away. As a result I was quite apprehensive about going to visit Warren H. Williams, the Aboriginal country music singer. He and his brother, Baden, were running late, so I had plenty of time to build up my anxiety. Eventually the door opened and two large, genial-looking men came in, followed by a pretty golden dingo with a pale belly and under-snout. Warren, the first into the room, looked straight at me: 'Oh, Doc Martin!'

They weren't only fans of *Doc Martin* but of *Black Adder* too. Laughing about those shows so far from home seemed surreal. I asked Warren the dingo's name. 'Aboriginal people believe they've already got their names, so we don't have to give them names. They know their own names.'

Baden chipped in, 'We laugh at the tourists who ask, "What's the dog's name?" It's not a dog, it's a dingo. What's his name? Dingo – that's it.'

It always makes me laugh when people get the sex of our dogs wrong. Often, when I tell someone Mary's name, they say, 'Aaaah! Isn't he sweet.' Just 'Dingo' seemed a sure-fire way of avoiding any misunderstanding.

We went outside, to sit on benches by a table on a wide brick terrace sheltered by a corrugated plastic roof and some trellising. There was a very unusual kind of garden, where grass had been swapped for red earth, and shape and structure were created by lines of pebbles. Where in England we'd have an edge of lawn or a bit of topiary, here there was a pile of rocks. The gum tree leaves made a dry percussive rattle in the breeze.

The dingo sat up between us. 'He's very aware what's happening, and he likes to meet new people and make new friends,' explained Baden. 'We got him when my big daughter was twenty-one. He's nearly two now. When he gets older he's gonna lose all the baby fat and look more muscled.'

The Aboriginal word for 'dingo' means 'from the bush'. Dingoes are territorial dogs who patrol the boundaries of their patch. When I asked whether the boundaries were drawn by man or dingo, Baden replied, 'A bit of both.'

'If another dingo's coming through,' explained Warren, 'they have a bit of a fight, then afterwards the dingo's welcome into the territory. The dominant male dingoes are the bosses of the territories, and when the pups grow up the young males are taught by the older dominant males about which territory is which.'

They're territorial, but independent too. 'Ours goes where he wants to go, walking around the community,' said Baden. 'We've trained him to be really friendly to black people and white people.'

'Yeah, he runs with our pack,' echoed Warren. 'He's the boss. The other dogs look at him with respect and back away when he comes. I've seen him head-butt a little pup, sort of saying, "Don't get uppity with me."'

In much the same way that Mary laid out the ground rules with Arthur.

'If the other dogs see him, they all go with him.'

I privately enjoyed the comparison with our dogs at home. Since we live on a farm the doors are open all the time, but Mary, Tina and Arthur are so stupid that they never go out on their own. The dingo sorts himself out when he needs to, whereas our dogs wait. Then, when they get a glimpse of sock, a glimpse of shoe, they jump up. 'Are we going out? Through the open door?' Yes, we are! All they have to do is step outside. Their need for human company is much more developed.

The Aboriginal view of the dingo conflicts with what Paul had told me. This was the third theory that had been put to me. As far as the Aboriginal people are concerned, there was no two-way movement that brought them together with the dingoes. 'Through Dreamtime, we're related to one another,' added Baden. 'This relationship has been going on a long time. Back home on the communities, dingoes belong to the country. A lot of the old people say, "Just leave dingoes where they are, because they belong to the land – they protect the land." '

'Dingoes came to us,' said Warren. 'All those years ago in Dreamtime, someone sent them to us for protection. They've never been a pet – they're just part of the family, like the kids. The same respect is given to the dingo as would be given to another person. A dingo's a playmate for the young ones, a companion for the older people and they act dumb with the others. You treat it as your kids.'

I couldn't help think of all the times I'd been criticised for doing exactly that with Mary. The words, 'It's a dog, Martin, not a child,' will probably go with me to my grave. But it seems to me that men and dogs look after each other's needs, so a dog deserves to be treated well. At that moment Dingo was lying panting on the table-top, quite content to have me scratch between his ears.

'We've got a brand-new car,' said Baden. 'He's always on its roof. He likes scratching it when he jumps up. When midnight changes to one o'clock in the morning, he howls and all the other dogs are really quiet. We have to come out of the house and say, "Shut up. We're trying to go to sleep." ' While we were talking Dingo had taken himself off to try out the roof of my hire car, checking his territory, scratching the paintwork and showing who was the dominant male. Like wolves but unlike domesticated dogs, dingoes don't generally bark. However, as I'd experienced, they do have a good strong howl. Warren explained that the dingo's howl stands out from the howls of the local dogs because it's still the howl of a wild animal.

As members of the family, dingoes, faster and stronger than humans used to help their people to hunt. 'Our ancestors were really good with spears,' said Baden. 'But if they felt a bit tired, they'd take a dingo out and show him where the kangaroo was.' The brothers told me that many Aboriginals use greyhounds for hunting these days, although they prefer the dingo because his stamina means he can run all day. Baden was adamant that dingoes only hunt in a pack if they are very, very hungry or threatened.

'I was working on my uncle's station with a friend of mine, a bull catcher who rounds up bulls and buffaloes with bull buggies [an old four-wheel drive reinforced with old tyres, steel plates and pipes]. There was a dingo in season and his pig dog [bull mastiff] wanted to attack the pack. I told that fella, "Don't let your dog go." And that fella said, "Don't worry. He used to kill pigs up in Arnhem Land." So he let that dog go and it launched into the dingoes. That pack ripped that pig dog to pieces and ate him while my friend was watching.

'But when they're by theirself, they're really good dogs. Really friendly. Once me and my missus took the kids to look for bush tucker – berries and that. There was a wild dingo on the horizon looking at us and a kangaroo not far from where we was. I had nothing, not even a rifle. The dingo came down and chased the kangaroo and killed him. He walked off and looked back at us, tail up, and walked off again. He more or less gave us that kangaroo meat for us to eat. We got it, cooked it up and ate it.'

Although Warren and Baden weren't going to be drawn about their ancestral beliefs, they were happy to describe life with a dingo in the family. Because the Aboriginal take on the dingo is quite the opposite to that of a white man, naturally their experience of living with a dingo was different. They painted a picture of an animal with an independent spirit, but one that added more to the family than just companionship

'Dingoes are different from domestic dogs,' explained Baden. 'They can understand what we say and they respond to our feelings.' They're protective and trustworthy family members: if it's cold they come really close and sleep with you. 'That's what those fellas are for – to keep you warm.' Baden talked about his two granddaughters, who are a couple of months old and a year old. 'He'll come and lie down next to the baby and won't ever harm her. If the one-year-old is walking outside, Dingo will run out into the yard and protect her wherever she moves. She can pull his ears and tail and he won't bite her.'

However, dingoes did sometimes have to be punished. 'If you smack a dingo when they do something wrong they go away, but they'll always come back. They don't bear grudges. You can say bad things to them and they'll just sit there and listen.'

163

These are far from the aggressive animals that we're led to believe they are. 'I remember the manager of the shop at Emmersbeck told me that there was a couple of Americans pulled up in a four-wheel drive,' said Baden. 'Dingo came out and they shut all the windows because they thought he would rip everything in the car. So the fella serving the fuel called, "Dingo! Come down here." The couple were panicking because they thought Dingo had run back to bite him. The fella said, "Don't worry about Dingo. He won't bite you – he'll just lick you to death." People think the bad side of dingoes, but they're not bad dogs unless you handle 'em badly.'

If a relative of the family dies in a far-off place, the dingo howls just once. The next day they'll always get the bad news. When someone's touched by black magic, has cancer or another incurable or serious disease, the dingo will urinate on them, marking them out for diagnosis. When they lick sores, they make them better.

Although they eat small animals and lizards, dingoes eat plants and berries too. 'They are more or less vegetarian, because they have to be. There's no such thing as a fat dingo. If he's fat, there's something wrong with him.'

Some white men might be sceptical about some of these attributes, but being there, listening to the two brothers and watching Dingo, I could believe almost all their claims. I wanted to believe the best of these beautiful animals.

There's no question that the Australian dingo is an unpopular creature with the farmers. But as Warren said, 'When all the people come with the sheep, it was easy picking for the dingo. You can't really blame him.' Because the dingo is such an important part of their culture, the Aboriginals don't support the culling pro-grammes. On the contrary, they believe that, 'If people kill a dingo, they get sick.'

The Aboriginal people revere the dingo. So many obstacles had been put in our way when it came to finding out more about them, but when we met Warren and Baden they were totally welcoming. All those thoughts distilled in my mind that night as we sat around the fire singing. It all comes back to the same thing: wherever you go in the world, there is a mutual attrac-tion between humans and dogs, and every dog's a winner.

II

Show Time

Dorset

'When it comes to my dogs, there are no holds barred'

Whenever I've been away, I always open the door to big smiles from Arthur and lots of wagging around from the other two. Coming back from Australia was no different. Although the fighting had escalated while I was away, it didn't ease off now the alpha male of the pack was back. My excited meet-and-greet immediately provoked jealousy between the cockers, so within moments of my getting indoors Philippa had to demonstrate the new technique of flipping Tina on to her back.

Instead of taking the screaming route (we've since learned that it's completely the wrong thing to do unless you want to whip your dogs into even more of a frenzy) Philippa now had something positive to do that seemed to work. Seeing her so empowered made me think we might be on the way to solving our problem. I had to verse myself in Cesar Millan's techniques. Philippa had watched all his programmes, but I contented myself with the highlights and soon picked up the idea. There's no doubt that it worked, but Mary caught us out a few times. She soon learned that we would intervene in any fight, so the minute we hauled Tina off her she'd redouble her efforts as if to say, 'I'm the chosen one, you bitch!' A couple of pairs of my trousers have been holed from her unexpected fighting back.

Otherwise we made a huge effort to keep checking and then blocking the bad looks between them. But however hard we tried, it was never enough. We lead such a chaotic life, what with all the other animals, Emily running around and us having to go away for our respective jobs, that it was impossible to prevent every fight. We made sure Emily understood that she wasn't ever to go near the scrapping dogs but was to get one of us to break them up. At least now we had some way of dealing with them when they occurred.

In the cottage there was a bottleneck where the one small door led in and out, and I was sure that it exacerbated the problem. As we watched the building work progress on the main house, we pinned our hopes on improved relations once we'd moved back. Unlike the cottage, it would have more than one entry and exit point: a big front door, a side door and a dog flap out into a little yard. Combined with the larger kitchen and underfloor heating, (so no competition for the spot in front of the Aga) things must surely improve.

The big excitement on my return was moving the horses from livery to our smart, new stable. Along with Bee and Saracen came Chester, my own gorgeous bay giant of a horse. I had bought him only six months earlier when I'd decided to take up riding again, largely in order to share some of the conversations of the rest of my family.

I learned to ride when I was a child; then, in my late teens when I worked at Theatre Clwyd, I would ride every day in the mountains. I rode with complete abandon, standing at a gallop and slapping the reins across the horse's neck. Once I was out with a friend whose horse's girth came loose. Our horses were picking up speed as they headed for home, and when she went ahead of me I saw her saddle slipping. As she fell in the direction of a dry stone wall (missing it, thank God), both horses took off like rockets. Not knowing what else to do, I kicked my feet out of the stirrups and threw myself clear. Fortunately the damage was no more than an agonisingly painful black-and-blue hip for each of us, but ever since I'd had the Fear.

Occasionally I'd been forced on to a horse for work. When Kristin Scott Thomas played my wife in *The Revengers' Comedies*, we had to turn up at a bloodhound meet on horseback. My steed kept wandering off its mark while we were talking, until it had to be replaced by a step-ladder. When we finally did a wide shot of the hunt, the master of hounds led off, blowing his horn. In the excitement my horse shot past him – considered very bad form – but because I was playing a posh shit I thought I could bluff it, so I yelled, 'Get out of my bloody way!' and off we raced, out of control. For me, the highlight of that film was lying down in a sea of bloodhounds, like a huge brown puddle of Clement Freuds. So much slobber. Heaven.

My other memorable equine encounter was in 2007 when I was filming *The Man Who Lost His Head* in New Zealand. Bethells Beach is right off the beaten track, despite being only a forty-mile drive from Auckland. The beach is wide and tidal, with a remarkable promontory of rocks on one side and beautiful sand dunes that swirl into different shapes. We shot a scene there where I had to ride a magnificent white horse named Shadow along the shore.

Shadow and I got on well. His friend George had been brought along to keep him company, and as long as Shadow could see George he was as good as gold. Unfortunately George wandered out of sight just as the director shouted, 'Action!', and Shadow bucked hard. I almost didn't notice, because I somehow landed on my feet beside him. I've never been able to do that again.

Despite Shadow being no stranger to this show-business lark – his CV boasted cameos in *Xena: Warrior Princess* and *Hercules* – I had wanted to try him out before filming began. So Philippa, Emily and I had the most fantastic two-hour ride. After trotting along the beach we turned our backs on the ocean and continued into the hills behind, through undergrowth into pure wilderness, unaided by tracks of any kind. This was the first opportunity the three of us had had to experience the thrills of riding together. That got me thinking, and big-hearted Chester was the result.

The dogs quickly adjusted to these three creatures who would take up so much of our time. After lessons to get me safely back in the saddle, I could ride out quite comfortably with Philippa and Emily. Whenever we can we all do lessons at a stables where there are a couple of wire-haired dachshunds (one of my favourite dogs) and a couple of deerhounds who ate the stable cat. Our own dogs don't get left out of the action, either. When we ride out Arthur accompanies us quite happily, trotting along a little too close to the traffic. Tina still affects disdain while Mary, after some initial uncertainty, just wanders in front, expecting everyone to get out of her way. I don't have ambitions to hunt or to be a dressage rider – I just enjoy riding for the sheer pleasure of sharing the experience with my family.

Discover Dogs is a show for over one hundred and ninety different pedigree breeds that includes the grand final for Scruffts, the nationwide competition for cross-breeds. We decided to make it a family affair, taking Mary, Tina and Arthur with us. We'd never been to such a huge dogfest before, although Philippa, Emily and I can be found glued to the TV when Crufts is on. Even Mary, Tina and Arthur, who normally show little interest in watching, join in. Once we did find Mary sitting on the sofa watching *Barking Mad*, a programme about problem pets, but she's never really watched TV since.

In 2007 we were completely hooked on Friends for Life, a Crufts' competition for dogs who have been heroes in some way or who demonstrate the friendship between man and dog. Suddenly the brushed up pedigree dogs that we'd loved up to that moment paled into insignificance beside these canine heroes who, brave and helpful, had proved themselves invaluable to their owners. The public were meant to phone vote for their favourite, but we thought they were all so fantastic that we voted for every one of them.

However, Discover Dogs was another matter. There were dogs of every variety wherever you looked, and plenty of stands making the most of the opportunity to sell every imaginable dog accessory or foodstuff. The exhibitors looked as if they were having a great time, brushing their dogs and preparing them for their classes. I loved meeting the more unusual dogs from the giant muscular guard and herding dogs such as the Bouvier de Flandre or the Giant Schnauzer, hunting dogs such as the Portuguese water dog, Irish wolfhound and Great Dane down to the Lakeland trail hound, an otterhound and a wire-haired dachshund, not forgetting the original lapdog, the pekingese, and the tiny fluffy Coton de Tulear from Madagascar. Even the last true new breed was there: the chesky terrier, developed about thirty years ago by crossing a sealyham with a scotty.

There are hundreds of breeds in the world, but the Kennel Club only recognises around two hundred in the UK. I was told that the Kennel Club has to investigate all

potential health and behavioural problems before recog-
nising a new breed, so it takes time for a new one to be
added. However, there are plenty of crossbreeds that
exist happily without formal recognition, such as the
labradoodle, the golden doodle and the cockerpoo. That
year, a three-year-old labrador/dachshund cross – don't
go there – was proud winner of the Most Handsome
Dog.

Walking around with three dogs, one of whom was
intent on tangling his lead up with everyone else's, was
hard. I was constantly anxious about how my dogs were
behaving. Impeccably was the answer – to the extent
that when Mary was sick, Arthur quickly ate it up. Our
director wanted me to enter Mary in the Dog Most Like
Its Owner class. A bit of a reach, I thought. And, indeed,
we were disqualified because it was Dogs' Day. So, no
rosette on sexist grounds. Arthur did a bit better by
winning second place, against hot competition, in the
Dog with the Waggiest Tail. His first rosette. And we
met Peter Purvis!

What interested me about the whole show, apart from
the sheer number of people and different breeds present,
was the fact that everyone, including myself, thinks
they're exempt from the ghastliness of the dog-owning
community that we're too lofty to subscribe to. The dog-
owners I met were completely dedicated to their particular breed of dog. It was almost as if, when they hit on a
breed to fill that vague dog-shaped hole in their life, they
began to support it as devotedly as others might support

a football team. When Arthur won his rosette I felt great, proving I'm just as silly as everyone else. You think your relationship with your dog is so special that it sets you apart from the rest of society, but in fact everyone else feels exactly the same about theirs.

Despite the thrill of seeing such a diversity of dogs under one roof and meeting their passionate owners, I still prefer the smaller, local country shows and fêtes. They're part of village life, not taken too seriously, and it's a terrific way to spend an afternoon a couple of times a year. People light up when you compliment their dogs. I do – I bristle with pride. Occasionally I'm asked to be a judge, which I love. I just respond to the way each dog makes me feel and award prizes accordingly.

I was once asked to be a judge in a fun dog show where the money raised was going to a local charity. When I'd accepted, the woman who'd phoned with the invitation said as an afterthought, 'You've got a dog, haven't you? Why don't you bring her along and enter her?'

'We'll only enter for a result,' I replied, without a trace of irony.

'Oh yes,' she said. 'I quite understand. We'll get a special rosette made up for her.'

Assured of success, we entered Mary in the Prettiest Bitch class, a category in which we knew she'd romp home. Emily proudly led her into the parade ring and Mary obligingly trotted round after her, looking head and shoulders the prettiest bitch there. When it came to the judging, the expert judge was one of Mary's vets – something we hadn't been expecting. Once seen in action, the entrants all lined up for a closer examination. The judges made their way down the line and, ignorant of our deal with the organiser and anxious not to make special allowances, gave Mary seventh place. Out of eight! What a travesty. Take my word for it that the other dogs were munters, including the lurcher that won. I confess that I've never done anything for that charity again and we never went back to that vet.

The next time, Tina was entered in a show where I was the judge. I had no hesitation in awarding her winner of the Waggiest Tail class. It may not be much of a tail but she can still wag it. I had no second thoughts about choosing her as winner. If I was judging and showed favouritism towards my child, I'd be a little embarrassed. But when it comes to my dogs, there are no holds barred.

Wherever I go, I'm always astonished by the vast number of breeds and crossbreeds. Four or five hundred years ago, most breeds would have been purely working dogs. Since then, no longer needed for their original duties, many have wormed their way into people's families. Seeing the wolves and dingoes had aroused a real curiosity to find out more about how all these very different breeds came about. Why don't dogs today all look like the wolf or the dingo?

As far as I know, no other single animal species encompasses such a vast range of individual character-

istics. Size ranges from the chihuahua to the Great
Dane. Ears go from the long and pendulous to the short
and perky. Tails and coats can be long, short, straight or
curly. The length of snouts and legs varies hugely.
Colours range over a wide spectrum of combinations
never exhibited by the wolf. How could this have come
about?

I knew just who to ask.

12

Playing God
Buckinghamshire

'By getting mixed up in genetics, and taking the breeding of dogs a step too far, we haven't always helped our best friend'

The Natural History Museum in Tring is a place with its own story. On his twenty-first birthday Lionel Walker, 2nd Baron Rothschild, was given some land on the family estate in Tring. Since childhood, when he had collected mounted insects, he had wanted to have his own museum. So, in two specially built cottages, he began a huge private museum of over four thousand stuffed and mounted mammals, birds, reptiles and insects from all over the world. In 1892, the museum was opened to the public for the first time. On his death, the distinctive Victorian buildings and their contents were bequeathed to the Natural History Museum in South Kensington. I went here to meet Bruce Fogle, a long-established clinical veterinarian and dog expert.

Of the six galleries, one is devoted to amphibians, bats, British mammals, domestic dogs, flightless birds, reptiles and small mammals. Among the narrow, slightly sinister corridors lined with large glass display cases crammed with stuffed specimens of different varieties of dog, Bruce was able to fill in many of the gaping holes in my knowledge of the species. I was impressed with his expertise as well as his ease in front of the camera. I was as unprepared for the extent of his knowledge, as I was for the stuffed animals. I thought I had already learned quite a lot about the subject, but time and time again I found his explanations clarified things I hadn't even thought of before.

In this macabre setting, as we walked past the eerily stiff, glassy-eyed dogs, I asked him whether man was solely responsible for taming the wolf. 'Mostly but not completely,' he replied. 'The dog is self-domesticated.' For thousands of years, most of the world had shared my assumption that the dog descends from the North American timber wolf or the European wolf. However, in the early 2000s research was published which showed that genetically the dog has no jackal, no coyote and no North American wolf ancestry. Dogs are descended from the smaller Asian wolf, brought to Europe when Asian peoples migrated across the Bering Strait between Alaska and Russia. 'These wolves took advantage of the new environment that human habitation created when we became agricultural. Wolves realised there were rich pickings by moving in on our campsites. The ones that survived were the ones small enough to live off what they could scavenge, because they were no longer catching large game. The humans had captured the large game.'

There's one school of thought that says dogs are stupid wolves. I belong to the school that says they're clever wolves. You don't see a wolf being brought its food on a plate. Who gets a blue cushion to sit on in the car? Seems to me that the domesticated dogs have got the right idea.

I spotted a medium-sized, short-haired dog with pricked ears that looked much like the dingoes I'd seen on Fraser Island. I was surprised to see how similar they were. 'This pariah dog is probably fairly close to the original dog,' said Bruce. 'There is DNA evidence that shows the pariah is very closely related to the wolf. If you compare its teeth to the Asian wolf, you'll see that they're more compacted. The brain is smaller because the animal no longer has a large territory to cover, so navigating territories was no longer so important. The intestinal tract is shorter, because it had a smaller variety of foods to eat. All those changes were due to natural selection, not to our intervention.'

Dogs are all members of the canine family that includes the fox, the wolf, the coyote and the jackal. But the range of size among the domestic dog is far greater than in other branches of the canine family. There are dogs that are smaller than the fox, and dogs that are bigger than the largest Asian wolf, such as the Irish wolfhound and some of the mastiff breeds. Although environmental pressures produced a smaller dog, there was always the potential for it to get bigger again. By intervening and selecting the bigger dogs to breed from, man could and did produce larger breeds. Close to the pariah dog stood a saluki, a tall, aristocratic-looking dog with long legs, head held high on a long, muscular neck. 'The DNA evidence shows that breeds like the saluki are very closely related to the wolf,' Bruce explained. 'The saluki is thousands of years old and probably getting closer to the size of the original Asian wolf, but these long legs and thick muscles are products of our intervention.'

Man accentuated the dog's natural potential to suit their needs. The saluki was bred to be a sight hound that would run faster than most other animals. Other dogs were allowed to survive because they too had qualities that man needed. For example, they might be the cuddliest (the smallest and most comforting), the fastest (for hunting) or the ones that barked loudest (for guarding).

We also intervened to make dogs smaller. By this time Bruce and I were standing by what looked like a perfect miniature greyhound, the Italian greyhound. 'This is a perfectly formed dog that happens to be very small. Initially, that would have been a genetic aberration. The dog would die off in the wild because something as little as that couldn't survive in the competition with the larger dogs. Through our intervention it survived because we liked it, for whatever reason. It didn't have to be able to help in the hunt. The reason could be as simple as a woman thinking, "I like it. It's not eating much food in the campsite, so what harm if I keep it?"'

Why suppose there was any difference between attitudes towards animals ten thousand years ago and attitudes towards them today? Apart from needing dogs for practical reasons, it must have been as much fun to have a little dog around then as it is now.

Dogs were developed for particular kinds of hunting. The basset hound is a scent hound with a long, sturdy body, big ears, a big, heavy-looking head but short, stumpy legs. 'Now that,' explained Bruce, 'is a dwarf. Dwarfism will happen as a genetic accident in any species, but when it happened in a dog, for some reason people decided to perpetuate it. Eventually the basset evolved – a ground or air-scenting dog that didn't run fast. If you were hunting on foot, this was the dog to go hunting with.' In contrast, standing close by was the elegant-legged foxhound that, as I'd often seen for myself in Dorset, was a fast pack animal that had enough speed to accompany the hunter on horseback.

One of my favourites was the dachshund, long and low, originally bred for hunting badgers in their setts – and good for them. If I had the chance, I'd be right up there with them. Those stripey bastards are the yobs of the animal world. They've dug up our tennis court, eaten the strawberries and carrots and knocked an apple tree over, and there's nothing we can do about them. They just swagger off with the nonchalance of a protected species.

Each breed that Bruce and I looked at had one aspect or another of their physical appearance altered so that they would excel in different fields. As these variants were developed and officially recognised, breed clubs were started and standards were established – not always in the interests of the dogs. A breed standard is the blueprint of a breed, against which all dogs in that breed are judged. Breed clubs initially set up standards that used extremes: 'as big as possible', 'as short as possible', 'as long as possible'. This meant that certain characteristics, such as the coat, the length of the legs or the shape of the head, would become exaggerated.

'Take the dachshund,' said Bruce. 'For a long time the UK and American breed standard said they should have legs as short as possible. So breeders started off with a dog like the one we're looking at, but at dog shows the dog with the shortest legs was going to win. The dog that won the show also won the right to breed. It takes no more than seven generations to change the form of a dog.'

I've seen for myself how some dachshunds have impractically short legs, so that their belly hangs too close to the ground. Of course, I was particularly interested in what he had to say about the labrador. The one we were looking at was lighter and with a less pointed nose than Arthur. 'To me, looking at that dog,' commented Bruce, 'that looks like a modern working labrador. Most of the labs that I see at the veterinary clinic are out of show lines and meet breed standards. They're built more like Aberdeen Angus bullocks, broader, with a flat back, quite muscular. When I go to Crufts and look at the labradors, the first thing that crosses my mind is that they're fat. This dog isn't. He's lean and well built. There's black-and-white evidence that the skinnier labs live longer. Research was conducted into eight litters born at about the same time. Half of them were fed as much food as they wanted, and the others were fed a very limited diet and were kept skinny. The skinny ones lived eighteen months longer than their fatter brothers and sisters.'

Pugs, originally from the Orient, are thought to have been brought to Holland for royalty. Genetic evidence shows that the pug is an ancient breed that was minia-turised thousands of years ago – how big can the original have been? Since then, they have been bred selectively to produce a face as flat as possible. Bruce told me that one of the most common operations that vets perform on pugs, once they reach physical maturity at about nine months, is to open the nostrils so that they can breathe. They also very often remove a little bit of the soft palate at the back of the throat to stop them snoring. These are problems that have been created by breeding to old standards.

In his essay 'Mickey Mouse Meets Konrad Lorenz', Stephen Jay Gould took illustrations of Mickey Mouse which showed that he began life with relatively small eyes and a sloping forehead, but within a few years his eyes became bigger and the forehead larger. Gould compared the most modern version to a caricature of a baby's head. Bruce pointed out that a pug's face is exactly the same. 'What makes it endearing is these great big eyes that trigger a primitive nurturing response in us.'

Apparently, pugs are an obstreperous, independent breed that, like other ancient breeds such as the Akita, Shar Pei and Shiba Inu, are among the more difficult ones to train. You have to work much harder with them than with the dogs that were selectively bred to work with us, such as the gun dogs. It's certainly true that we didn't have any trouble teaching Mary, Tina or Arthur – all gun dogs – the basic commands of sit, stay and come.

We haven't restricted ourselves to changing the physical dimensions of the domestic dog. We've played around with colour and temperament too. Until there was a breed standard poodles came in parti-colours, so you might find a black and silver one or a black and apricot one. Since the standard was established, poodles come in single colours only – black, brown, apricot, champagne, white. 'Every now and then,' said Bruce, 'a parti-coloured pup crops up in a litter. Thirty years ago, it would have been drowned because it didn't meet breed standards. Now, they're intentionally being perpetuated simply because people like them.'

The terrier was another breed he picked out as difficult to train. 'If it's just got you and it's concentrating on you, then yes, easy to train – sit, stay, come. But show it something small moving and it forgets all of its training. Its instinct will take over. Of course, every dog's natural instinct is to chase anything small that moves, but terriers have been selectively bred to exaggerate their aggression. We didn't inject the killer instinct but merely enhanced the inner wolf that lurks there even today. Terriers are much more aggressive than the wolf. If they see anything that looks like prey they'll kill it, whereas a wolf will kill it only if it's hungry.'

Over the last twenty years, certain European mastiff breeds such as the Pyrenean or Bernese mountain dog have become very popular. Yet once they were known for their aggression and unreliability. 'I wouldn't have wanted to be alone in a room with one in the late 1960s or early 1970s,' Bruce said. 'But they look like gentle giants – and now, that's what they are. The breeders modified the dog's behaviour by selective breeding. They didn't breed from aggressive dogs and they did breed from gentle dogs. Only seven generations later, their behaviour had changed but not their looks. These were dogs that served one function, and now they have a totally different one. Today they're companions, members of the family. That's a perfectly valid function for a dog, but it's quite different from the function they were originally developed for.'

One important factor in breeding any ideal dog is genetics. The Bernese mountain dogs look like giant teddy bears, but they can develop serious medical problems as the result of being bred from a small genetic stock. 'The founder stock is very important in breeding. These were originally simply bred to guard and protect in mountain pasture. When they were brought to Britain, it was in the time of quarantine regulations. As a result, very few were used in the original breeding and unfortunately some of those few carried a predisposition for cancers. They develop these cancers when young, and that's why their life expectancy is so short.'

So by getting mixed up in genetics and taking the breeding of dogs a step too far, we haven't always helped our best friend. It's extraordinary to think that the greatest dog breeders ever were alive between five and ten thousand years ago, when many of the breeds we know today emerged. But, for the time being, I'd heard enough theory about dogs and breeds. I wanted to get out and see some of the oldest working breeds in action.

13

Company for Killing

Dorset

'They like doing what they're bred to do – hunt.'

I first became aware of our local hunt when Emily joined the local Pony Club and came home wearing a sweatshirt with 'CATTISTOCK HUNT' on it. I was taken aback to see an eight-year-old with those words on her front – not what I'd been used to! Until then, I'd had no idea that the Pony Club was affiliated to the local hunts.

The first time I'd seen the hunt in action was the day the people from the TV company involved in making *One Man and His Dogs* came to Dorset to meet us. As we stopped to open the gate there was the hunt behind us, cantering along our top field – a wonderful sight to behold. In our last house I'd always been worried for Mary because she was fox-coloured, and I'd pick her up when that local hunt was around, just in case!

These days, of course, foxes are no longer the quarry. Since 2005, when foxhunting was banned in the UK, hounds have been adapted to hunt a fox-based scent instead of the real thing. The huntsmen reproduce the same conditions as in traditional foxhunting by laying trails in the same areas, in the same sort of direction and using the routes that foxes used to run.

Never having been to hunt kennels before, I was looking forward to meeting the hounds at close quarters. I felt there was something historical and impenetrable about the sport of hunting. Although I'm English, it's always been alien to me. As you approach the Cattistock Hunt kennels, you hear the hounds barking before you smell them. Outside, I stopped to admire some lively six- to eight-month-old hounds who were standing on their hindlegs by a fence, claws clinging to the wire, pleading their innocence Guantanamo-style – no orange jump-suits, obviously. As soon as they saw me they rushed the netting, jumping up, pushing each other out of the way, eager to say hello. I stayed there for a moment, scratching ears and chins through the wire.

Charlie Watts, the huntsman, met me at the gate. He's a man who, if he was a dog, would be a lurcher: wily, knowing and confident. 'When the pups are anything between ten weeks and six months old, they're sent out to "puppy walk",' he explained. 'We've got people around the country who take two or three puppies for five or six months to teach them their names, a bit of obedience and about life in general by introducing them to other people, farm animals and traffic. They're in-telligent dogs, so when they get back they live out here until they're mature enough to come into the kennels.

Before that, we introduce a few of them at a time to the kennel and exercise routines. They soon pick them up and take on board that I'm the boss. To begin with they follow me around the fields, and then, during the summer, we exercise them on the road. It's all education for them, and the younger hounds begin to learn off the older ones.'

Charlie walked me through the back entrance into the kennels, a narrow but spotlessly tidy yard surrounded by white-painted brick buildings with postbox-red woodwork. A very distinctive gamey smell came from the kennel, quite different from that of a domestic dog. As soon as the hounds heard Charlie's voice, they went silent. Every early morning in the hunting season they follow a strict routine, but on a hunt day they aren't fed for twenty-four hours beforehand. 'We're taking out fourteen and a half couples today [Thursday] and they haven't had anything to eat since Tuesday evening. But they're fed on raw flesh [dead racehorses, other horses or male calves] that takes between twenty-four and forty-eight hours to digest, so there's still something in them. Nobody can take exercise on a full stomach, and hounds are the same.'

I knew I would love the hounds before I saw them. From a distance, the hunt makes an impressive and mystifying sight to a former townie: the horn, the red jackets and the baying hounds. Foxes have been hunted for centuries. As deer became more scarce and foxes became a countrywide problem, huntsmen adapted the hounds' hunting ability so that they would recognise and track the scent of a fox instead. The first properly recorded foxhunt in this country took place in Norfolk in 1534, with the first hunts, the Bilsdale and the Quorn, founded in the seventeenth century. At the end of that century, the Reverend W. Philip of Cattistock Lodge in Dorset started the True Blue Hunt, later renamed the Cattistock Hunt.

Before going to the meet, Charlie and his team let the hounds into a nearby field for a five-minute run out. At the entrance to the kennels they go through a footbath containing salt and formalin or copper sulphate, which washes their feet so that cuts are disinfected and grit gets washed away. If a foot is badly cut the salt stings, making the hound limp. Charlie will spot it immediately and deal with the injury.

As he opened the gate to the kennels the hounds came thundering out, legs flying everywhere. There's a real weight to their footfall that I'm not used to with my dogs. I stepped out of the way just in time and watched as this ocean of hounds flowed past me. Charlie was carrying a long whip.

'It's not for hitting or correcting them. It's to control them. When we're on a road and a car comes, we stop to let the car pass. If I hold the whip out in my right hand, the hounds will get over to my left side. They always watch to see what I'm doing and where I'm going.'

As we walked into the field the hounds charged up the hill, though several hung back to say hello, jumping up, and one in particular loved having his chin scratched.

Dorset, a black hound, stood to one side, barking vociferously. He didn't like my being there one bit. The others were more confident and friendly, or else took no notice of me at all.

Because there was so much variation in their ages, colours and coats they looked like different breeds of dog, but they were all foxhounds. Some were about eighteen months old, in their first season, some were in their ninth or tenth season. Some were parti-coloured, others single-coloured – black, brown, tan, cream or white. Some had short sleek coats, while others were coarse and wiry. The one thing they all had in common was that they were bright-eyed, alert, fit and strong.

'The rough-coated ones have a bit of Welsh foxhound blood that goes back three or four generations,' Charlie explained. 'The dark-coloured or black ones and gingery ones have got American foxhound in their blood. We've got four or five different lines of American breeding that goes back ten or fifteen seasons. We sent one of our bitches to a pure-bred American stallion hound. She produced so many puppies that we've been breeding from the offspring down the years. The American hounds have a tremendous amount of enthusiasm, although their conformation – their look – is slightly different. They tend to be taller, lighter and slightly faster than the English hounds. They've improved the hunting ability of our pack tremendously. We had a lot of criticism for introducing American blood, but they're all congratulating us now.'

When you're looking to the breeding side of things, there's a lot to consider: hunting ability, conformation and character. For instance, all that barking counts against Dorset. 'We probably wouldn't risk him siring a litter,' said Charlie. 'He's too timid. Chorus, that dark, wiry-coated bitch, has got some Welsh and some American in her breeding. It's OK to experiment with these out-crosses, as they're called, but they must gel with the rest of the pack.'

Thinking about the difficulties we had with our dogs at home, I was surprised to see how well the hounds seemed to get on together. They live as a mixed pack with the males kept complete. When the bitches come into season they're separated off, then reintroduced to the pack three or four weeks later. 'Mixed sexes live better together,' Charlie said. 'You rarely get mixed-sex fighting, although occasionally things might get a bit grumpy between a couple of dogs or bitches.'

No comment.

Where we get all that vying for the position of top dog at home, the hounds live and work as a team with perhaps two or three of them doing the best work on one day and another three or four on another. The only time any trouble flares up is when they're fed. 'Maybe there'll be struggle to get the best or the most meat,' Charlie told me. 'But they soon learn that thirty seconds spent arguing over a bone or a piece of meat is wasted. By the time it's over, another hound has eaten whatever it was they were fighting over.'

Although Charlie was obviously proud of his hounds and knew every one of them by name, he didn't touch them. 'I treat them all the same,' he explained. 'If I was going to stroke one I'd want to stroke them all, and time doesn't allow. Like I said, they respect me as their leader. Until they're hunting, when they become their own leaders, I'm in charge of them and they know that. On a hunting day, all they're looking for from me is to take them to the area we're going to hunt and to find the trail. Then they hunt the trail themselves.'

I asked Charlie if he had any favourites. 'I love them all to bits really. There are some that are really out standing in their work or their hunting ability.' He pointed out one or two. Chadwick, that one having a rest, he's a good dog that I'm really pleased with. Cornwall, that tan one, is an exceptional hound that we'll hopefully use as a stallion hound when he's older. Then there's German. He's about ten, in his ninth hunting season, but he still keeps up with the youngest. He's been a good working hound all his life and he's sired two or three really good litters. But they're all favourites really.'

Despite my experience with Angus, I wondered whether a properly trained foxhound might make a great pet. Charlie disagreed. 'My wife wouldn't entertain having one as a pet. They're big and boisterous and they need so much exercise. Besides, kennel routine and the hunting instinct has been bred into them for three or four hundred years.'

Those who work with them insist that these are not dogs, but hounds – it's a standard correction given to inexperienced townies like me. But there is no sub-species here. They are still technically dogs, and when I stroked them and made a fuss of them they responded like any other dog. They did, however, seem more in touch with their instincts. And, by the way, those jackets are definitely red, not pink!

I watched as they gathered round Charlie, all eyes on him, tails wagging, waiting for his next instruction. At one word from him, they raced back into the kennel where they waited until the horse-box was ready to take them to the hunt. When the time came, they quite happily crammed into one end of it – the box was then partitioned off to make room for the horses as well. They had been through this routine countless times and knew exactly what was in store.

The meet was held in the corner of a field, with a farmhouse near by and the Dorset countryside rolling away into the distance. All the usual followers were out, about a dozen of them on horseback with a few on foot. It's always good to see the horses, beautifully turned out, snorting and stamping with impatience to get going but waiting while their riders, smart in their hunting gear, down a stirrup cup or two. There was a definite sense of occasion. It was a bright but cold November day, so I was glad when someone put a drink into my hand and a cocktail sausage into the other. This is a good system.

The hounds were milling about, sniffing the ground, avoiding the legs of the horses, picking up the air of anticipation. After twenty minutes of waiting, they had reached fever pitch and were bursting to go. Charlie was there, of course, looking quite different in his 'pink' coat and hunting stock, waiting to give the signal, 'Hounds, please' so that the hunt could move off. Despite his having claimed he didn't favour any of them, I spotted him kissing one of the hounds on the nose. There's no real difference between professional and recreational dog owners – they're all soppy. At last the hunt went off, the hounds chasing ahead, noses to the ground, as Charlie led them to the woodland where the trails had been laid. He was planning to follow three or four trails that day, so the pack would probably be out till dusk. The hounds were expected to cover thirty or forty miles at varying paces without running out of stamina. Five days later, hounds would be taken out again. One or two of today's hounds might join the second pack when they went out on Saturday as well. They are tireless animals.

I was sorry to hear that two days later Charlie's twenty-seven-year-old horse, Laddy, whom I had admired out hunting, had sadly died.

Much the same as undertaking, ratting is an everyday business but one unknown to most of us. Plenty of people have trouble with rats and there are all sorts of ways of getting rid of them, but using dogs is as good as any – quick, green and surely preferable to poisoning.

I'd been surprised when Bruce Fogle had told me that terriers were bred up to be fiercer than wolves, so I was intrigued to see this other traditional breed of working dog in action. By the time I reached the farmyard where I was expected the rain was teeming down, but it wasn't dampening the spirits of Midge, Scruff and Stan, three very excited Jack Russells who were waiting for me by the open-sided barn. With them was Johnny, the rat-catcher. I don't mean to be insulting, but the word 'Dickensian' sprung to mind when faced with his appearance, job title and job itself – which is a million miles away from most people's experience. As I met the terriers, Johnny surprised me by telling me there was no such thing as a pedigree Jack Russell. 'That's why they're such fun, because you never get two the same. You get all sorts of shapes, sizes, heights – long-legged, short-legged – and colourings.'

Midge and Scruff belonged to Johnny and were mother and son. Stan was borrowed for the day. He had a duelling scar on his nose from a previous encounter with a rat and was already barking, rushing about, digging his nose under the straw. All three of them were alert and keen to work, with pricked ears and wagging tails.

Just by the straw, there was a pile of animal feed. The farmer had already lost half a pallet to the rats. At fifteen pounds a sack, something had to be done. Apart from eating feed or grain, rats present a threat to humans because they carry leptospirosis or Weil's disease in their urine. Humans can catch the disease from contact with contaminated water or through a cut, the mouth or the eye. If left untreated, the disease can be serious or even fatal.

Johnny's mate, Andy, was here to help, fresh from a culling expedition in South Africa. I didn't ask what was being culled, but it seemed horribly appropriate. He revved up the tractor once the dogs had been put back on their leads to avoid accidents. For them to get at the rats, Andy was going to have to move several of the bales at a time. He and Johnny had put wooden barriers round three sides of the barn so that the rats only had one exit route. Somewhere under the straw they were squeaking, aware that something was up.

The dogs were straining at their leads while Andy moved the front lot of bales. The rats would run further and further back towards any remaining cover, but as Andy gradually removed more of the straw they'd be left with nowhere to go. 'One or two might try to break out, but once the last two bales are left I'll let the dogs off and see what happens.'

Suddenly the dogs were free and shot forwards towards the remaining bales. I ran back almost as fast, as a sea of grey rats squirted out in my direction. I saw one young rat get away and inwardly cheered, 'That's it, you run'. The dogs were on to them in a flash and the kill was fast and furious. The terriers shook each rat until its neck broke, then went quickly off after another. Lifeless, they were of no interest. Johnny piled up the corpses out of the way while the terriers went back to the chase.

'Once they've been bitten a couple of times, they realise that they've gotta kill 'em quickly,' said Johnny. 'For instance, if they caught one by the back quarters, it would just turn round and bite 'em, latch on to 'em. Once they get bit, they get more aggressive. They don't need an awful lot of training to get the hang of it.'

Three rats had escaped into the field. They were probably sitting there, smoking roll-ups until the coast was clear. Johnny reckoned that they were every bit as intelligent as pet rats. He told me the story of being called in to catch a rat that had got into somebody's house. He went into every room but couldn't see it anywhere. The dogs went mad, chasing around the house, but with no more luck than Johnny. Then, 'I looked up and there it was. It had climbed up the curtains and was sitting on the curtain rail in the bathroom, watching us. We were looking everywhere for it, and it was up there all the time going, "You can't see me!"'

The reason Jack Russells make such good ratters is down to their size but also to their nature. 'They're fearless and they like doing what they're bred to do – hunt. They won't back down to anything. If you had one the size of an Alsatian, you wouldn't be able to control the thing.' Johnny had obviously got a couple of good ratters in Midge and Scruff. 'The best we did was one hundred and eighty-three in one and a half hours. They were underneath two chicken houses. That was a bit of sport.'

A nineteenth-century Englishman, Parson John Russell, developed the breed specifically for chasing foxes out of a den without harming them. Today there are two strains, the Jack Russell and the Parson Russell. The breed probably split early in its history when it's thought the sister of Russell's kennel man sold some small terriers that she described as 'Jack Russells' although they may not have been part of the line bred by the man himself. The longer-legged Parson Russell is now a standardised breed, whereas the genetic soup of the non-standardised Jack Russell is so muddied that when you breed from two of them you can never predict what the pups will look like. I like them for that.

With the growth in organic farming less chemical rat killer is used, so the Jack Russell has become an organic alternative – although a farmer would have to keep several of them if they were going to make a difference. But not only are they efficient ratters, they make great pets too. 'They're pocket-sized, you see. Don't take up too much space.' The only problem might arise if there was a clash of domestic interests. 'This one, Scruff, ate my daughter's gerbil. So goodbye, gerbil,' laughed Johnny. 'It's just the nature of the dog. Something little and furry they're going to kill. I can't take Scruff out with my ferrets – it'll kill them. But Midge will run around the garden playing with 'em.'

As we talked Scruff was nosing at the pile of dead rats, picking one up and crunching on it, making sure it wasn't going to run away. Having double-checked, he dropped it like a toy that had lost its battery. Meanwhile, Stan and Midge were chasing around the remaining bales, scratching at their bases in the hope of getting underneath, then racing around over the top of them, frustrated by the sound and smell of the rats. Once again Johnny called them, putting them on the lead while Andy removed the remaining bales. If the rats had gnawed through the baling twine, the bales might split apart and fall on the dogs.

Once they were off the lead again the dogs ran everywhere, quite obviously loving every moment of their work. More rats ran for cover, but the dogs were too quick and these were added to the growing pile of corpses. Usually, seeing the extinction of any life moves me, but I had mixed feelings here: I love dogs, and these rats were vermin. Midge, Scruff and Stan were so business-like, and it's clearly such sport, that I couldn't condemn them. Like the working hounds, they were doing what they'd been bred to do and doing it with efficiency and joy. At one moment, those perky, snouty little terrier faces were looking up as if they were smiling – the next, they were killing machines.

14

The Oldest Profession

Cumbria

'Training a sheepdog is something like starting a fire. If you blow on the flames too hard, the fire goes out; similarly if you come down too hard on a dog, it will refuse to work again'

The farmer who keeps his sheep on our land has four sheepdogs, three border collies and an Australian kelpie, which I watch with admiration. The way they round up sheep looks to me like super-controlled chasing that can only be put down to an unmatchable and enviable bond between man and his dog. I've spent my dog-owning years studiously teaching all my three dogs not to chase sheep – they'll all chase a sheep if it's running. Arthur now comes back when I call, but there was a time when his interest in them was definitely more than just friendly. Dogs have been used for herding for as long as they've been put to hunting or guarding. I'd seen how hunting dogs were put to work, so I was intrigued to see how man had harnessed dogs' instincts all those years ago to make a good herding dog.

In Cumbria I met Derek Scrimgeour, who has been breeding, training and working sheepdogs for the last twenty years as well as farming sheep on his fifteen hundred acres. He told me that one of the worst days of his life was the one when he had to round up his entire flock so that the army could shoot them during the 2001 foot-and-mouth epidemic. For a week or so afterwards he questioned whether to give up this way of life, but then thought better of it and spent the next four years building a new flock to match the one that had been destroyed. Leaving his farmhouse and the warmth of the Aga to a scatty, lamb-like Bedlington, a litter of Westie pups and Derek's wife, who was baking and making soup, we headed outside. Derek looked exactly the part in a Barbour and flat cap, carrying a crook. The snow still tipped the peaks of the surrounding mountains, although it had melted from the hillsides. A little way up the nearest open slope were scattered a dozen or so sheep.

From the moment we had left the farmyard Fleece and Drift, the two dogs which he was using today, were looking up to him, waiting for his command. They don't share the family home but are well housed in barns and kennels with the other sheepdogs being trained or bred on the farm. While Fleece trotted beside us, five-year-old Drift was kept on the lead. He is such a keen dog, I was told, that he would get bored while we talked and go off to 'gather the hill' by himself.

I'd never thought of a sheepdog as a potential killer. But as Derek explained their aptitude for herding, I began to see them in a new light. 'If these dogs were in a pack hunting, they would be herding the sheep into corners so that they could kill them. When you see the sheep enter the pen at a sheepdog trial, and the handler closes the gate, the dog's thinking, "Why doesn't he kill them now we've got them in there?" That's the point when some of the dogs get a bit frenzied and zip round the back of the pen and try to bite the sheep. You can see the instinct when they're stalking. It's the same with the big cats.'

He sent Fleece, a three-year-old black smooth-coated bitch, away across the open field where we were standing towards the sheep. As I watched her responding to his commands – waiting, moving to the right, stopping, moving to the right again – until the band of twelve or so sheep were herded down the hill to us, her killer instinct looked well under control. 'Fleece is one of a few dogs that are such naturals at the job, it's as if they've already been trained in another life. Her brothers and sisters are quite ordinary, but she's a special dog. Fleece is a genius compared to me,' explained Derek. 'She's naturally good and learns so quickly. I've trained her from the start, and it feels as if she almost talks to me. She picks up in minutes what other dogs would take weeks or months to learn.

'With these dogs it's all in the genes', he went on. 'If you've got a dog with a strong killing instinct, it's no good. If you've got one whose instinct isn't strong enough, it will be frightened of the sheep. The balance has to be right. A dog needs to have enough of a desire to kill that it unnerves the sheep so that they move away from it, but not so much that it terrifies them.' Breeding is crucial, although you can zip up a tentative dog or cool down a more aggressive one in training. However, it's impossible to breed to order. 'This bitch is really special.' Fleece's eyes never once left him as he spoke. 'She's got a lot of talent and she's kind to the sheep, but she's got power over them. But . . . she could breed a killer just as easily as she could breed a good dog. There's no guarantee.'

When Derek was a child living on a hill farm in Scotland, he became terrified of dogs after one bit him. His mother bought him a collie pup in the hope he'd get over his fear. That pup was the start of his lifelong involvement with the breed whose cleverness still amazes him. Having been a shepherd first in the mountains of Scotland and then at Lonscale Farm on the rugged Lakeland Fells where he breeds his Killiebrae sheepdogs, he knows exactly what makes a good working animal. Temperament and stamina are all-important. 'If they've got the stamina, that looks after the conformation and muscle tone.'

Training a sheepdog is something like starting a fire. If you blow on the flames too hard, the fire goes out; similarly if you come down too hard on a dog, it will refuse to work again. When a dog shows an instinct to work, you have to mould it carefully. After two years of training a dog, Derek can tell whether or not it's going to make the grade. Most of them do, because these days the real killer instinct has largely been bred out of them.

212

A dog's family lines can indicate whether they've been bred to be more or less aggressive.

Border collies are different from other dogs. They've been bred for generations as underdogs, so the shepherd is always the boss in the team. For that reason Derek would never breed from a dominant collie. 'All you have to do to dominate a collie is to step in front of it and say, "Come on, let's go," and you're the boss.'

Collies born without a working instinct make better pets than those that want to work. The addictive side of their nature needs to be channelled elsewhere or they will find themselves something else to do – and it won't always be something the owner wants.

Out of the eight or nine litters that are born each year at Lonscale, Derek often keeps one or two of the pups to see how they turn out. People have different ideas about how to pick a puppy. Some think a good dog should have black roofs to their mouths or three hairs under their chin, but Derek's not convinced by that folklore. You might as well close your eyes and pick at random from a litter. There's no way of knowing the nature of the dog until you start training it.

Thinking about Mary's hip dysplasia and the problems that labradors can get in their joints, I wondered if there were any weaknesses inherent in this breed. Derek told me that a small percentage have eye problems, but breeders eye-test all the potential parents just in case. Over the last couple of years, too, he told me, potential buyers have asked for the parents to be hip X-rayed in an attempt to avoid hip dysplasia. 'But the important thing is the quality of the dog,' Derek insisted. 'You can get a perfect dog with perfect hips and perfect eyes, but it doesn't work. You can plan litters, but some of the best dogs I've had have come from random unplanned ones.'

Derek doesn't keep bitches to breed repeatedly. 'I hate the idea of shutting them up to breed from. They come, they have a litter and then I train them on and they go and have a life.' We went to look at his latest litters, black-and-white sweeties snuggled up under incubating lights for warmth.

The dogs start to work between six and eight months old, when they begin to want to chase and round up sheep. 'I usually get some quiet sheep and let the dog play with them. Right away you'll see whether you've got a killer or more of a herding dog. All I do is protect the sheep, staying with them, using a hard voice, as well as trying to block the dog and defend the sheep until the dog realises that I don't want him to attack them.' He uses a harsh voice when the dogs aren't moving well and a nice, warm, open voice when they are doing exactly what he wants. These dogs love praise, and work in order to be rewarded by that note of approval and encouragement. By rewarding the dogs with the sound of his voice, Derek gives the animal a freedom that allows it to make its own choice as to where to go. 'If they don't stop upon command, they hear an angry voice. The minute they stop, they get a calm voice. The more they obey, the nicer the voices get.'

All his Killiebrae sheepdogs are trained to respond to the same basic traditional commands that have been used for hundreds of years. ' "Come by", and the dog goes left. "Away", and it goes right. "Lie down" means stop. "Walk on" tells them to walk forward. "That'll do" is the command for them to come back, and "Look back" asks them to turn around to see if any sheep have got left behind.'

Nearly every sheepdog handler still uses these commands, although just as important are the whistles that vary depending on the handler. 'It's whichever whistles you can manage best. You've got to make sure that your whistle can be raised in volume to carry over a mile.' Putting his fingers to his mouth, Derek showed me how he could control Fleece by using whistles with rising or falling notes to match each of the basic commands. 'You're the pack leader, and all you're doing is harnessing the dog's instinct. The whistle is clearer and more logical than shouting, so the dogs work better on the whistle.'

With some sort of pride, I told Derek that the sheep farmer who uses our land has four dogs.

'They can't be much good then,' he retorted wrily. 'If they're any good, you only need one.'

I'd imagined a stereotypical gruff shepherd, but Derek had a real gentleness to him. I hadn't expected to find a man who was so clearly in tune with his dogs: his eyes lit up when he was talking about them. 'Somebody once asked me if I loved my dogs. My reply was, "No, I don't – but I really respect them. Especially the good ones." Drift is a nice dog, quite clever, but he needs me more than Fleece does. He's the son of one of my dogs, but someone else reared and trained him. I bought him to sell, but I liked him so much I kept him. I liked his style – honest, straightforward and uncomplicated. That's how I like my dogs. I'm using him as a stud dog now. I have a fifty-fifty partnership with Drift. With Fleece, I think I'm only about twenty per cent of the team. She'll run a mile to fetch sheep for me.'

I was impressed by Fleece's obedience and skill as Derek worked with her to bring a small flock of sheep in our direction. I could see how she was using just the right amount of pressure to move the sheep without scaring them. They still had time to graze a bit as they moved towards us. Derek watched her like a hawk, so that if in rounding up two stragglers she missed the balance point and lost control of the rest he could help her. 'Mostly I leave it to her natural instinct to fetch them back to me, but if I can help her then I say something – otherwise I just leave her alone.'

As well as breeding the dogs, Derek brokers them. 'Some dogs grate against your character, just like people. But if somebody gets a dog that doesn't fit them, they sell it, and eventually they all get matched up with someone who gets on with them.'

Because it's so hard to get good dogs, many British farmers now use quad bikes or motorbikes to herd their sheep, or else they attract them with buckets of feed.

Dinky, the singing dingo, is a nationwide hero in Australia. Just don't mention the h*** word.

Warren and his pet dingo who, he told me, held equal status with other family members. That's as it should be.

To try and calm the fighting down, we added Arthur Colin, to the mix. He's wonderful, but he hasn't helped the fighting.

The photo below was taken by Lord Lichfield for the 2006 PDSA calendar. When it was published, Tina's breeder Jean Ormes yelled at me for her bad hair!

Charlie Watts, the huntsman, knows every one of his hounds by name and tries to treat each one the same.

When the hunt passes our house, I always pick Mary up, as she's so fox-coloured, just to be safe. Charlie Watts pictured here, on the far right, riding Laddy.

Andy, left, and Johnnie with Stan, Midge and Scruff. An unregistered breed, no two Jack Russells are ever the same. One thing was for sure, these three really enjoyed their work.

Not bad going in under an hour.

Sheepdog Drift's eyes never once left Derek.

I hadn't realised that all Derek was doing was harnessing the dog's desire to kill the sheep.

I adore judging dog
shows, seeing all the
different dogs out
there . . . as long as
my own dogs win.

Pictured here at
Discover Dogs.

Meeting and greeting at
Nettlecombe Dog Show.

These bulldog puppies were gorgeous, but the truth is the adults can suffer many health problems.

Still the best way to clean a saxophone.

That may work well in a small field, but Derek couldn't farm his fifteen hundred acres of rugged Cumbrian hill pasture without his dogs. The terrain is too difficult to negotiate on a bike.

Over the last fifteen years or so, plenty of people who aren't farmers or shepherds have taken up sheepdog trialling as a hobby. Derek trains people with their dogs, taking around two years to train up a good-quality dog. And now it was my turn. Both Fleece and Drift were very intense, yet biddable, as I found out when I put myself to the test. Drift, Derek promised, would listen to anyone – and he did. For a moment the thought crossed my mind that our land is good grazing land, and if I had the right dog. We could feasibly have our own flock instead of letting a local sheep farmer rent the fields. Then I remembered that I had a job, builders and a wife, none of which or whom would tolerate it. Back to reality. Told to imagine myself on Drift's rough white back as if I was on a horse, I had to give my instructions in relation to where he was and what he was looking at.

'One of the worst things you can do is shout,' Derek warned. 'All that does is tell them that you're annoyed. It doesn't give them any information. They're so easy to confuse and so quick to guess. If you don't give them any sort of sensible advice, they start to guess and then you're in trouble. You've got to keep it controlled and logical.'

If I wanted to slow Drift down or was in doubt about what to do next, all I had to do was say, 'Lie down', stabilise him, and then start again. I had to remain in control of what was going on, by giving commands at a speed that Drift could take, or else he would take over. 'The rule is when you stop him, you start him. Don't let him start on his own,' Derek warned. 'Once he knows what you want he'll be much easier to control.'

All this was more easily explained then done. I couldn't help feeling that having a Scottish accent might have helped me. The problem was, I didn't really know what I wanted. I got Drift to bring the sheep nearer and nearer to us, but once we were surrounded I lost control and had to ask for help. It was a far cry from puppy class.

I asked Derek whether he thought any of these techniques would translate to the dogs back at his house – or at mine. 'None. Terriers don't want to be bossed. They want to *be* boss. The Westies are responsive, but if I try with the wire-haired fox terriers they just give me a real hard look as if to say, "What are you doing?"'

These sheepdogs were a breed apart: beautiful to watch at work, and certainly the most biddable of the dogs I'd met so far. Their instinct is to chase sheep, and where the wolf in them would kill these sheep they're trained to know that that's bad form in a sheepdog. Out of breeding, training and competing, Derek admitted to getting most pleasure from being out on a hill on his own with a dog, just doing what a dog's supposed to do. 'If you spend a day with a good dog, it's like being with a friend. It's great.' Exactly.

15

Facing Obsolescence
Kent and Goodwood

*'Although many of the traditional working breeds
continue in their roles in time honoured fashion, others
no longer have a purpose at all'*

O ut of all the cocker spaniels I've ever met, not one of them has been used for their original purpose of hunting. Mary and Tina's ancestry stretches right back to the fourteenth century, when the larger spaniels were used for springing game and the smaller ones for flushing out woodcock from the undergrowth. Bred for its neat, compact body, thick coat and soft mouth, the cocker was only differentiated from the springer by the Kennel Club in the late nineteenth century. By the 1930s, the cocker was the most popular dog in Britain. Somehow, along the way they had outgrown their prime function and become the best household pet there is.

Although many of the traditional working breeds continue in their roles in time-honoured fashion to a greater or lesser degree, others, such as the Irish wolfhound or the otterhound, no longer have a purpose at all. Another is the great British bulldog.

Bull-baiting was a national sport in England from medieval times. A bull was led into a rope enclosure, where it was firmly tethered to a post by a rope either around its horns or from a collar. The dog's role was to approach the bull, seize it by the nose (the most tender part) and not let go. These were originally mastiff-type dogs, chosen for their courage, strength and ferocity. The better they were, the more money could be made from them. The dog owners realised that, to be certain of winners, they needed to out-breed from the original fighting dogs. They deliberately bred a dog that was fit for purpose, with the majority of its weight around its head, so that its back was less likely to break when swung around by an angry bull. The appearance of the bulldog has changed little since. When the sport was outlawed in 1835, the breed would have died out but for a group of bulldog fanciers who adapted it to keep the look but to modify the personality. Given bulldogs' history, I wanted to find out how much of their dogness they had kept.

Peacocks and peahens strutted across the immaculate front lawn of a splendid two-storeyed timbered Tudor house complete with jettied top floor. The heavy front door was flanked by statues of bulldogs – one *couchant* (French!), one on its hindlegs pushing a wheelbarrow, another standing in a traditional bulldog outfit – a sure giveaway to the preoccupations of the owner. I'd come to meet Alison Barnsby, a breeder since 1979 of Britain's favourite mascot – the English bulldog.

222

I was welcomed into the house by Dandy, a bulldog wearing a union flag coat in my honour, Carmen Miranda, who sported a coat covered in tiny union flags, and of course their owner, Alison. She showed me through a creaking door into a long, beamed living room with leaded windows and a stone fireplace at the far end. On the floor in front of the fire and between the two sofas was a large wooden whelping box where eight five-week-old bulldog puppies lay on a sheepskin rug, looking like a box of creamy-coloured slippers.

Curious to see their new visitor, they waddled, squeaking, over to the edge of the box, tumbling over one another as they tried to stand on their hind legs. I picked up Spot, a chubby white pup with a black spot over one eye. Like all the rest, he had big paws and plenty of loose skin to grow into, a flat black button nose, wide-set eyes, tiny flaps of ears and the makings of those distinctive bulldog jowls – not forgetting that peculiarly leeky smell that all pups have. Have you noticed that the breath of all puppies smells of chopped leeks?

Dandy was brought in to be stripped of his vest so that I could see a prize-winning bulldog conformation. As she spoke, Alison turned the obliging Dandy around to demonstrate the different features developed in the interests of baiting bulls. 'They're a thick-set, middle-sized dog that has a pear-shaped body, bred so that the shoulders are tacked on to the side of the ribcage instead of underneath, as in most dogs. His legs are strong and straight. His ribs are barrel-shaped, so they break less easily than a flatter rib-cage and they allow plenty of room for his lungs and heart. The position of his legs allows him to drop his ribcage between his shoulders, so he can creep towards the bull with less risk of being caught by the horns. When he's close enough he springs up and gets the bull by the nose.'

Her arms round Dandy, she turned her attention to his head. 'The bottom jaw projects in front of the upper jaw so he can latch on to the bull. His neck is short and strong so the bull doesn't break it by tossing him around. If he does lose his grip, he's thick-set and well boned so that he doesn't get hurt easily in a fall. His nose has large nostrils and is set back so that, when he's got the bull, he can still breathe. The wrinkles channel the bull's blood away from his eyes, and his ears are little so they don't get in the way. He doesn't need them, in the same way that he doesn't need a tail to balance him. A perfect tail would be a little straight carrot of a tail.'

So, a designer dog – but what a design! The breeders had paid astonishing attention to detail, right down to the facial guttering to drain away the blood. I had no idea that a dog's conformation could be changed so specifically to serve its function. But there's a downside too. Being bred for a large head and narrow hips can cause many bitches problems when giving birth – the pups' heads may not fit through the pelvis. Caesarian births have consequently been very common for this breed. Alison felt that a bitch must be very confused when landed with a litter that she has no sense of having given birth to.

After bull-baiting was made illegal, the dogs were bred without the aggression needed for attacking bulls but leaving other typical traits such as courage, a high pain threshold and that stubborn character. 'These are very laid-back people dogs,' insisted Alison. 'But if you cross them with, say, a terrier or boxer, and lose the temperament, then you've got a cross that could be a bit scary. The only breeds recognised by the Kennel Club are the bulldog and the French bulldog, a slightly smaller dog than this with tulip-like ears. You do see people advertising Victorian bulldogs, Regency bulldogs, Sussex bulldogs and Old Time bulldogs, but these are really crossbreeds that aren't formally registered.'

People began to experiment with these different crosses because they felt that the standard bulldog had become too heavy and was not as healthy as it should be. Among other things, the shape of the face meant that it had difficulty breathing and the wrinkles around its eyes encouraged infections to take root. These new crosses are bred to be lightier, skinnier and taller, with longer, less wrinkled noses. However over the last thirty years, in the face of this cross-breeding, standard bulldog breeders have been working in conjunction with the breed council, who have now devised a health assessment test for all breeding stock to encourage the production of healthier dogs.

'Bulldog breeders try to breed within their own gene pool to keep the temperament,' explained Alison. 'If you cross it with other breeds you risk losing that. The breeding standard has been changed to emphasise the health issues – so, for example, the neck should be 'moderate' rather than 'short' in length. The tail has always been straight, but people now breed them with a curly tail. Some people think that's cute, but if it twists round and gets hot and sweaty it's not very nice having to clean it with a baby-wipe. Again, healthier eyes are encouraged in the breeding stock. Nice open nostrils make it easier for them to breathe.'

The puppies had scattered in their box but then Alison let in their mother, Blondie, a white bulldog with small brown spots and a larger one over her right eye. Immediately her offspring rushed to the edge of the box, stepping on each other in the anticipation of food and squeaking with excitement. Blondie stepped rather un-enthusiastically into the box and the pups latched on before she had even had a chance to sit down. After a moment or two, clearly fed up with the whole mother routine, she stepped out again, ignoring her pups who fell off the teats. Alison was particularly proud that this bitch had given birth naturally. She assured me that Blondie wasn't being a rotten parent, but some of the pups had by now developed sharp teeth and so feeding them wasn't as comfortable as it had once been! This was nature's smart way of getting the puppies to wean themselves. Alison had assisted the process by offering the puppies scraped steak when they were about two and a half weeks old. At five and a half weeks they were almost completely weaned, and Blondie was going to get that figure back.

Meanwhile, without attention focussed on him any longer, Dandy went and cocked a leg against one of the chairs – not for the first time.

For some reason, these engaging but not the most attractive dogs have become the one seen as emblematic of our dog-loving nation. Bulldogs have been synonymous with Britishness certainly since the nineteenth century. At the outbreak of the First World War Winston Churchill, then first Lord of the Admiralty, compared the Royal Navy to the British bulldog. During the Second World War they appeared on posters encouraging people to contribute to the war effort, and statuettes were made giving Churchill the face of a bulldog because dog and national leader shared character traits and there was a certain facial similarity. The Young National Front has called its journal *Bulldog*. Alison thought it must be because 'They're what we like to think we are: brave, courageous, loyal – and with a lot of flatulence too!'

I had noticed, but had been too polite to say anything.

'One thing about bulldogs is that they're not a dog for people who want a dog to do exactly what they tell it when they tell it,' Alison continued. 'They will obey in the end, but if they don't want to they'll make very hard work of it.' Suddenly I saw a characteristic that was

227

horribly reminiscent of my cockers. I hadn't noticed any reluctance to obey us until we had Arthur, who in contrast is so eager to please. I was recently told that a labrador is born half-trained and a cocker will die half-trained.

In the next room lay Atomic Kitten, proud but tired-looking mother of three twelve-day-old pups who pummelled her teats with their feet to increase the milk flow. While they guzzled, Kitty rested her head on a cushion, an expression of benign resignation written all over her face. One pup had been born naturally, but the other two had tried to rush into the world together and so the vet had been called to perform a Caesarian. In the wild, mother and pups would have died. Even though the litter had survived thanks to timely veterinary intervention, there were still difficulties. 'This little one is a useless sucker,' said Alison, indicating one of the litter. 'She messes around and makes much more noise because she hasn't got a strong suck. If she was a wolf cub the other two would probably push her out, but I referee and make sure she gets her fair share.' So saying, she moved the pup to another nipple with a better milk supply.

Alison's obvious enthusiasm for the breed is impressive, and there was no doubt that she worked hard to produce the best dogs she could. I did think her disappointment that these three pups had curly tails spoke volumes. Over the fireplace hung a picture of Beaudiddley Doc Martin, the handsome father and mascot of the Tring Rugby Club, looking down at his brood. At matches he wears his own rugby strip, which prompted me to wonder how much the bulldog breed gets dressed up in general. Alison confessed that she made her own costumes. 'The most elaborate so far was a "wolf in sheep's clothing" with a fleecy body, legs and a little tail. I was gutted when we came second to a hot dog.' There was nothing I could say.

Alison tried to convince me that, despite what seemed intrinsic physical disadvantages, bulldogs were none the less fun-loving animals. 'They're more of a sprinter than a marathon dog. They'll run for short bursts of about a hundred yards,' she said. 'I think different breeds play differently. Bulldogs enjoy using their strength, barging into things, squashing things and flattening them. I did have one who played butting with our goat. He never worked out that the goat had the advantage over him.'

However loving and dependable a pet the bulldog makes, they did seem to me to have lost something of their essential dogness. Alison described to me how they loved going for a walk – but only for ten minutes or so. That's all their laboured breathing will allow. It's impossible to imagine them running for the sheer joy of it. I thought of Mary, Tina and Arthur or any of the other working dogs I'd met, their zest for life and the pleasure they get in chasing each other or racing along a stretch of beach or through a field. By comparison, these dogs seemed slightly aimless, standing in a room not quite sure what to do with themselves. I'm just not sure that, having been genetically engineered with such care, the dog is always the winner in terms of quality of life.

Where a traditional English breed such as the bulldog was rescued from possible extinction by its followers and fans, another ancient and exotic breed from overseas was saved from obsolescence in its own country and brought into England – all thanks to a few dead eunuchs. Their role was purely to be house pets or lapdogs. Nowadays we have many more, such as the Shi Tzu, the Lhasa Apso and the Chinese crested dog, but I was interested in finding out more about the one that began the craze: the pekingese.

On 23 February 2008, the Duke of Richmond welcomed one hundred and thirty pekingese breed enthusiasts to his stately home, Goodwood in Sussex, for a champagne reception and black-tie dinner before the pekingese championships to be held the next day. While the festivities were going on, ninety-three pekingese dogs were curled up in their baskets somewhere near by. The event was to celebrate the close connection between his family and one of the oldest breeds of dog in existence. Both the Duke and Brenda Oades, secretary of the Pekingese Club, met me before proceedings began to tell me the extraordinary history of the dog.

The representations of the pekingese in ancient Chinese art suggests that their pedigree stretches back over two hundred thousand years: they were carved at temple entrances and appear on rare porcelains and tapestries.

The breed's origins are steeped in legend. One myth holds that when a marmoset and a lion fell in love, the lion begged Buddha or the god of animals (depending on who's telling the story) to shrink him so that he could mate with its new love – the result being the pekingese. Others claim that a lion had been shrunk for the same reason when it fell in love with a butterfly. Though he was now small, the dog retained the heart of a lion, its boldness and courage. Buddhists certainly believed that the lion embodied the spirit of Buddha, and it's thought that monks of this religion may have wanted to create a lion-like dog. Known as the lion dog, and believed to be a gift from Buddha, it was a breed unique to the Chinese imperial court where it was revered as semi-divine. During the Tang Dynasty, a thousand and more years ago, they were regarded as royalty themselves and looked after by eunuchs. The emperor would select four dogs to accompany him on state occasions. Two would go in front and announce his approach with a bark, while the other two carried the hem of his robe in their mouths. Anybody found injuring them or stealing them faced the death penalty.

The dogs were at the height of their popularity in the nineteenth century, when breeding was undertaken with the utmost care. Bitches were shown pictures and sculptures of the best-looking dogs, and favoured colours were hung in their sleeping quarters in the belief that it would influence the appearance of the litter. They slept on sheepskins to encourage their coats to grow. White animals were particularly prized and kept as temple dogs.

The pekingese came west in 1860, at the end of the second Opium War, when the British and French stormed the imperial Summer Palace outside Beijing. There, in a remote corner of the garden, the British soldiers found five pekingese, abandoned by the Emperor's aunt who had committed suicide after hearing of the advance of the British forces. They were brought back to Britain where two, Schloff and Hytien, were given to Admiral John Hay who in turn gave them to his sister, the Duchess of Wellington. General Hart Dunne presented a fawn and white one, Looty, to Queen Victoria. The remaining pair were given by Sir George Fitzroy to his cousin, the Duke of Richmond and Gordon. This was the first pair of breeding pekingese in this country, and the start of the Goodwood strain. It's believed that they bred for forty years with an unbroken line. Meanwhile in China, the powerful Empress Dowager Cixi owned and bred pekingese prolifically until she died in 1908. She presented a small black peke named Manchu to US President Theodore Roosevelt's daughter, Alice.

The Duchess of Richmond's daughter-in-law, Lady Algernon Gordon Lennox, became a champion for the breed and it was she who introduced new blood into the line. In 1896 Mrs Douglas Murray imported two famous pekes, Ah Cum and Mimosa. The story goes that when Lady Gordon Lennox spotted her with these pekes in the street, she ran after them. As a result of that meeting Ah Cum was mated with two Goodwood bitches to produce the 1898 champion, Goodwood Lo.

Lady Gordon Lennox was one of the founding members of the Pekingese Club in 1904. Then, after a row over weight issues, in 1908 she set up the Pekin Palace Dog Association for breeders who supported the smaller pekingese that weighed under ten pounds, which they considered the 'palace type' as originally looted from China. These can in fact weigh as little as five pounds or less, and are know as 'sleeves' because they were small enough to fit up the loose sleeve of a Chinese traditional costume. Under seven pounds, they're known as 'miniatures'. The two clubs maintained different breed standards until 1949, when the Kennel Club insisted there should be a single defining breed standard.

The Duke told the story of Lady Gordon Lennox giving a pekingese to a foreign ambassador. A year or so later, she met his deputy.

'How's the little peke?' she asked.

'Madam,' he replied, 'it was delicious.'

Brenda assured me that, despite the long hair and short legs, these dogs are every bit as doggy as the next breed. 'They chase sticks and balls. They chase ponies. They chase anything if they can. They don't need much exercise, although people do take them for walks every day. One I sold went out hunting with labradors, so they can keep going if they want to.' These dogs are generally perceived as lapdogs, kept by the aristocracy – although Brenda assured me that the lapdog idea is a fallacy. Some love nothing more than being petted or stroked, while others don't want to know and would rather be on the floor, independent.

There was a phase in the first half of the twentieth century when the dog was particularly popular and the breeding standard demanded flat faces. Now, however, the snouts are longer again and breathing is easier.

Brenda has bred pekes for years. I asked her what it was that drew her to this breed over any other. 'Each one has a completely different temperament and personality. They're independent characters although, like any dog, they are trainable. They're basically just a fluffy, pretty dog, same as any other breed, although they are the most regal breed that exists in my opinion.' Theirs was definitely the best breed story I'd come across so far – and still the most efficient way to clean a saxophone.

16

Buried Alive
Yellowstone Park, USA

'Older occupations may have died out or be less popular, other new and sophisticated uses for dogs have been found'

Buried under the snow in a small man-made chamber, I pulled out my hip flask and took a swig. My exit route had been sealed by one of the Yellowstone rangers, who was now tamping down the snow on the outside so that the rescue dog would have to use her nose and not her eyes to find me. I was going to have to lie here for at least fifteen minutes until I was freed. I paused the videocam, aware that I was beginning to talk drivel like everyone who's asked to make a video diary, watched the *Dad's Army* film on my iPod and drank more whisky.

Our relationship with dogs has evolved in various ways over the centuries. While some of the older occupations may have died out or be less popular, other new and sophisticated uses for dogs have been found. The point of this rather extreme game I was playing was to see some of the Western Montana search dogs, based in Yellowstone Park, in action. Earlier I had met their uniformed owners, Colette Daigle-Berg and Bonnie Gafney. Wrapped up against the heavily falling snow, I was introduced to Sula, Colette's six-year-old border collie mix from a shelter in Polson, Montana, and Auggie, Bonnie's four-and-a-half-year-old German shepherd.

Both Sula and Auggie have been family pets since they were pups but they have also been expertly trained as search-and-rescue dogs, always kept physically fit and exposed to all kinds of situations from riding snowmobiles to agility training and tracking, retrieving and searching exercises. 'We count on them and we rely on each other,' explained Bonnie. 'You'll see that the bond between dog and handler is the most important thing. They have to want to work with you. The drive level is high, but they have to have a trust in you.'

Search dogs have been used for centuries, but their training has been continually adapted and refined. St Bernards have been used in the Swiss Alps since the eighteenth century, when the Augustinian monks took them up to the St Bernard Monastery high in the mountains above the St Bernard Pass. The most famous of all St Bernards was Barry, born in the monastery in 1800, who is reputed to have rescued at least forty people until his death in 1814. His stuffed body is displayed in the Natural History Museum of Bern, complete with keg of brandy round his neck – although the keg was probably a myth perpetuated by a beady Victorian brandy manufacturer.

Since then, the work of these early dogs has been expanded on and different dogs have been trained to suit different types of rescue. Today's rescue dogs tend to be lighter in weight than the original St Bernards; most commonly used are German shepherds, border collies, labradors and golden retrievers. All these breeds plus rottweilers and scores of crossbreeds provided the backbone of the search-and-rescue operations at the site of the World Trade Center disaster. These extraordinary dogs are frequently in the news: recently they were brought in to help the police in the searches for Madeleine McCann, for victims at the Jersey orphanage of Haute de la Garenne, and for bodies and survivors in the Chinese earthquake. In Italy, Newfoundlands have been trained alongside labradors in sea rescue. The dogs leap from helicopters with their trainers and, attached to a rope, swim with a lifebuoy to people in trouble. A dog can often reach people in situations out of a boat's reach.

All over the world, air-scenting and trailing dogs are used in wilderness, water and disaster searches. Airscenting dogs pick up traces of human scent that are floating in the air, while trailing dogs follow minute particles of human tissue or skin cells that have fallen to the ground or on nearby foliage. In Yellowstone, the dogs are a prime example of this sort of work. 'Like many of the dogs in Montana, our two are crosstrained,' said Colette. 'That means they're not only trained in avalanche rescue but also in water recovery,

239

cadaver and drug detection, tracking and trailing. Dead or alive, people emit gases or smells from their body cells. The scent rises through the snow or water, and that's what the dog is trained to smell.

'To train them, you have to like dogs and you have to like being out in all weathers. But what really makes it fun is that the work is a team effort. The dog has the nose, but we need to direct the dog into the wind so it can catch any scent on the wind currents. We direct and put the dog in the position to find the person.'

Colette and Bonnie were both business-like about what they did, and didn't big up their sidekicks as anything special. They were obviously dog lovers and were more than happy for me to make a fuss of both dogs, who were lovely, affectionate creatures. Once out of the car and seeing their owners wearing their back-packs, they knew they were going to work. Lying under the snow, I was hoping they would prove as good as their press.

To demonstrate the training, three mounds of snow had been dug on the open hillside. 'We want it to be an exercise for the dogs so they don't go straight to the mound,' explained Colette. I was to hide in a chamber dug in one of them, constructed so that it wouldn't collapse. Before I lay on the snow and reversed myself in I was equipped with a radio, so that I could communicate with the outside world, and an avalanche transceiver that sends a signal that can be picked up by a search team carrying the corresponding receiver. If everyone wore these devices and knew how to use them, perhaps there wouldn't be such a need for dogs.

'Sometimes we train for fun using transceivers,' added Bonnie. 'We use them to compete with the dogs. The dog always wins. But if we were skiing together and one of us was caught in an avalanche, then without my dog your life depends on me being able to get out my transceiver and locate you.'

Bonnie agreed with Colette that working with bitches was personal preference, not a must, but she added, 'I'm training my second dog, who's a male. These are high-drive dogs, and if I had two males the competition between them would lead to fighting. It's all about harmony at home.'

No comment, again.

Five minutes must have passed when I thought I heard the sounds of feet over my head. They went away. Lying in that tiny space, I could believe how grateful you would be for a dog's arrival in a genuine snowdrift. Sadly, most of the people recovered aren't in a position to appreciate their discovery because they're dead and the dead are notoriously unappreciative.

At last, I definitely heard Sula above me. This time she was barking. Now digging. I was praying she wouldn't bring the whole thing down on me. As she dug, the chamber got less and less dark. Then, there she was. Colette was with her and thrusting a dog toy into my hand so that I could reward my rescuer. Sula squeezed into the hole with me so that I could make a good old fuss of her. Colette had explained that in training it's a good thing for the 'victim' to keep the dog in the hole and play with her. The trainers want their dogs to feel comfortable in the hole, not afraid of going in there. Each discovery must be finished with a game as a reward, something not always easy for the friends or family of the dead to witness.

Apart from practising with willing bodies, the trainers also practise with items that might get lost in an avalanche: backpack, jacket, skis. Any of these might give a clue to a victim's position. While burying a few of these, they had put human scent all over the hillside to make it more difficult for Sula who now had to distinguish between the different scents. The snow was packed hard on top of each item. Bonnie explained, 'Most avalanche debris is set up pretty hard and you can move around on it easily. The dogs would get worn out if they had to flounder though thick snow, but packing the snow down also disperses the scent.'

Once I'd extricated myself from my hole I watched Sula bound across the snow, stopping, nose down, then moving on. Then she'd start to dig frantically, snow flying everywhere, until she'd dug out one of the buried items. Every time she found one, Colette was there with the toy, playing with her and congratulating her. What I loved about these dogs was that, however trained and hard-working they were, they were still full of *joie de vivre*. You somehow expect a working dog to be bespectacled and bookish in its endeavours, but I was glad to see they were dogs celebrating being dogs and we've managed to make that work for us.

That night I got back to my hotel to find a message from Philippa. Despite her success using the Cesar Millan approach, our warring cockers had stepped up hostilities again in my absence. She'd been unable to divert Tina in time, and yet another ferocious scrap had ensued. I'd been worried that this might happen, because there's often a shift in the group dynamic when I go away. At least when we were both at home, there were two of us to break them up. Once again Philippa had had to weigh in alone, and in pulling them apart had been bitten a couple of times on her arm. I was relieved by how calm and in control of the situation she sounded. Being bitten must have come as less of a shock second time round. By now, we knew that was the risk in keeping the dogs together, although we always hoped that the last fight would be the last ever. But it never was.

When we finally spoke, we discussed what other course of action we could take that might not involve constant attention that was impossible to give. I remembered that I had met Sarah Fisher while she was chaperoning her two daughters, Emily and Daisy, when they appeared in an episode of *Doc Martin*. I'd mentioned to Emily (hers not ours) that we had two cockers who fought and she simply said, 'My mum can fix that, it's what she does . . . mainly horses, but she does dogs too.'

Sarah's a highly qualified equine and companion animal instructor as well being expert in something called TTouch, described by her as using 'a system of gentle, non-habitual movements of the animal's body, including the skin, to promote relaxation whilst improving awareness, physical balance and movement'. She had left us a note with her phone number, offering help if we ever needed it. At the time we hadn't followed it up, not really understanding what it was that Sarah did. But we had reached a point where we felt we had run out of the more traditional solutions. Jean, Tina's breeder, still thought we should get Tina a new home. But we had made up our minds to keep her. Philippa agreed to contact Sarah and arrange for her to visit us when I was back home again. Meanwhile, there were still dogs and people for me to meet in the Yellowstone area.

For Christmas 2004 we'd taken Emily to Lapland to meet 'The Man'. While we were there we went on a midnight husky safari, the girls wrapped in furs as I did the 'mush' thing, standing behind them on the treads of the sled. It had been a magical experience with the cold wind on our faces, sleigh bells, candles in the pine trees, stopping by braziers to drink hot chocolate, picking up enough speed to get the girls screaming, and much more fun than the reindeer ride we'd had earlier in the day.

Thirty miles north of Yellowstone, in the foothills of the Absaroka Mountains, I met Mark Nardin, owner of Absaroka Dog Sledding. An earnest man, knowledgeable about his subject, he had driven to meet me with a trailer-load of fourteen huskies that we were going to harness to two sleds and drive through the Gallatin National Forest. But before going anywhere I needed a lesson in the nuts and bolts of sledding. I bit my lip, saying nothing about Lapland.

Mark has run his business for twenty years, using the dogs to take tourists through the Park and for racing. 'Mushing', or driving a dog team, originated in North America and Siberia, where the native Inuit and Chukchi used them for pulling loads. The Siberian dogs were smaller and faster than their American counterparts, so were exported to America during the nineteenth-century gold rush.

Mark keeps ninety-six dogs in his kennels: currently seventy-five working adults, some retired and some of the next generation. He maintains the number by adding new dogs when others retire, which they do when they stop running as fast as the other dogs – whatever age they have reached. Mark lets the dog dictate its own terms. Everything Mark's crew do with their puppies is a step towards being on a team. 'Initially nothing's asked of them: the pups are just petted while they smell who it is that's giving them comfort. Through time more voice tones are introduced, and by the time they're six months old they come out of the puppy pen, to have a collar put on them and be given a spot in the main kennel. By the time they're a year old, we put them on the gangline that connects the harnessed dogs to the sled and go down the trail for the first time.'

Having three dogs at home can be problematic, but

ninety-six is taking the mickey. Consequently, these dogs live together in a 'dog lot' where all the dogs are kept on a chain. 'People think that's negative, but in fact it's a benefit because they learn how to step over, duck under and so on,' said Mark. 'Yesterday, I was punching a trail open after a bad snowfall and I ended up with six dogs in a tiny space because the snow was so deep. My leader turned round and looked at me, like, "Do we have to go any further?" I was, like, "Yes, you do." So they proceeded to extend themselves out, a couple of them stepping over and under to stretch out the gangline.'

Mark was very clear about his alpha role in their pack. 'The main thing for a musher is to provide them with all the care they need, and in return they give me the miles I'm asking of them. I look at my dog team like a little league baseball team. If I manage by intimidation, I lose productivity. If I manage with positive reinforcement and they all have fun, they just might exceed their potential.'

The important thing for a musher attempting to communicate with dogs is to use a language they under-stand, using one of the three different voice tones they use themselves. 'They have a bark to warn, a growl to intimidate and a yap to play. So if I fluctuate my voice in those tones, the dogs will know whether I'm giving them a command, scolding them or happy with them,' ex-plained Mark. 'Women are good in this sport because they've been taught nurturing skills. If you've been around a lady very long, I'm sure you've heard the words, "I don't like the way you said that." That's how we have to interact with the dogs. Say what you mean and mean what you say.'

Trained teams of dogs can cover one hundred miles a day, depending on the terrain, the temperatures, how far they're going and the loads they're carrying. If there was snow on the M1 and beyond, a pack could drag a sledge the entre length of Britain in seven days. When training, Mark tries to get his teams to keep to about eleven miles an hour over a hundred miles in a twenty-four-hour timeframe. 'That's not asking too much of a team. Some mushers will run them slower and some faster, but those arc the numbers I feel comfortable with because I don't want to violate the dogs' trust in me. They know I'm not going to take them to fatigue point.'

Mark was training a team of dogs to enter the qualifiers for the Iditarod Trail Sled Dog Race. Also known as the Last Great Race on Earth – by those who take part in it – it runs from Anchorage, in south central Alaska, to Nome on the western coast of the Bering Strait. Each team of twelve to sixteen dogs and their musher cover over eleven hundred and fifty miles in ten to seventeen days. The race originated in 1925, when there was a diphtheria epidemic in Nome. The Alaska Railroad Hospital in Anchorage had enough serum to save the situation, but it had to be got to Nome within two weeks. The train took it to Nenana, two hundred and twenty miles north of Anchorage. Beyond that, they had to rely on the dog teams that delivered bundles of mail to the outlying communities. Dogs who already know a trail will get from point A to point B whether it's daylight or night-time or white-out conditions. They won't quit. A relay of dog teams carried the serum six hundred and seventy-four miles to Nome in the remaining time and the epidemic was taken in hand.

These dogs are so loyal that they'll just keep going until they can't go any further. Their stamina is second to none. A musher's skill is to make sure they're asking enough of the dogs but without asking too much. The crucial thing is to remain detached from the other competitors and focussed on the terrain and your dog team. 'It's like being in a racing car and worrying about the cars behind you. They're irrelevant.

'We like to run them all night long because dogs are nocturnal predators. Like the wolf, they're going to be doing most of their hunting in the pre-dawn hours. A dog team will cover more miles between 2 a.m. and 7 a.m. than they would between 2 p.m. and 7 p.m. As a musher I want to make it as easy as possible on my dogs, so it's better to get them working in their natural time zone. Working them later would be like asking you to work at three in the morning. You might be there, but you're not going to be very productive, whereas if you were there at 10a.m. you'd do better because that fits your time schedule. It's pretty special to be out all night long, watching meteors flash through the sky with the snow illuminated a bright blue. The dogs show us things we never get to see without them, and sometimes just seeing them out on the trail is special enough.'

The Boston Police Department K9 Unit was a seriously impressive act to watch. This dog actually bit me on the ankle.

These amazing hearing dogs came in every shape and size. But all undeniably noble.

A big name.

Meeting a legend.

Life on the farm
in Dorset.

Tony Fitzjohn built Mkomazi out of the dust. It was Tanzania's first rhino sanctuary. Now he's set up an African Hunting Dog breeding iniative there. Being a part of releasing the pack into the wild was a huge privilege for me.

Of all the dogs I've met, these are quite different. More independent and wary of man than any other species. Quite beautiful.

I helped with drugging and attaching a radio collar to one of the soon-to-be released dogs.

Tony's latest friend, Tomtoliki.

Children and dogs. It just works . . .   And puppies too, of course

Before getting the dogs out of the trailer, the sleds and harnesses had to be prepared. Mark makes his own sleds, kiln-drying an imported hardwood because the local pine is too soft, then treating it so that it will bend into the shapes needed for a sled. The sleds are based on a Native American Athabascan design with narrow slats and a high curved handrail at the back behind the seat. They're very light in weight. Mark laid out the gangline and showed me how to harness the dogs to it.

For the sledding we were about to do, he was going to get the dogs out one at a time, harness them and attach them to the gangline. A warning: 'These guys can get pretty loud out here. They're like second-graders going out to recess together, and the anxiety level gets pretty high. But as a musher I'm looking for that – otherwise it would be like a parent having to wake their child on Christmas morning, and that's not natural. I also use the noise as a barometer to tell me how the dogs are feeling. If one of them got sick last night, I'll find that out here and I won't take him out.'

Before the dogs were let out, he gave me detailed instructions on how to drive the sled and avoid the dangers of falling off or having the dogs take off without me. It was hard to take him too seriously when I knew we weren't going to be travelling far or fast and there was plenty of snow to land on. This was hardly going to be the Iditarod Trail. Besides, I knew he and his team would be in front of me, so my dogs wouldn't be able to run very far.

249

At last it was time to bring out the dogs. Today he had two different types: Siberian huskies and Alaskan huskies. 'The Siberian is a true Arctic but the Alaskan is basically a hybrid mutt. If you look at the Siberian husky and the wolf, you'll see a lot of communality there too. They're all running animals and used to running mile after mile, day in, day out. Their abdomen and ribcage are tapered down toward the breastbone and, much as you would see in a wolf, they have a tucked up loin. They have a long back they can extend out with their neck and back vertebrae in line, and most of them will have their tails extended to a certain degree. Our kennel emphasis is maintaining the Siberian husky as a working sled dog.

'The Alaskan huskies came about during the days of the Klondike gold rush in the Yukon and Alaska. During that time, dogs from the west coast of the United States were taken from Los Angeles to Seattle, where the miners used them as a means of transportation. They don't look like a sled dog, although they have a similar skeletal structure to the Siberian husky.'

The first out was Junior, a beautiful Siberian husky from Alaska. I could definitely see the wolf in him. The first command Mark gave him was, 'Harness.' He immediately knew something was being asked of him. Then 'Step.' Junior lifted a foreleg, to be rewarded with a scratch on his chest from Mark as his head and then the raised leg went through the harness. Another 'Step' saw the other foreleg through. 'That's what I'm looking for. When I have twenty-six or twenty-eight dogs that I have to harness myself, the dog will cooperate as much as the dog can.'

I thought the dog's spirits might be deflated by not being able to run free, but they were alert, with tails wagging, and obviously eager to get going, I stood between the two lead dogs as Mark and his helper harnessed up the remaining four on my team and the eight on his team. As each dog was brought out the sense of anticipation mounted, and those already harnessed were straining at the lines, wagging tails, barking and howling, keen to be off.

After such a build-up, the ride was pretty anti-climactic. No bells, no candles in the trees, no hot chocolate, no real sense of fun. We crept along in little or no danger, following a trail edged with snow-covered pine trees with Mark and his team going smoothly ahead of us. My favourite part of the trip was when the cameraman, Richard Ranken, and I flipped out of the sledge and lay laughing in the snow.

17

Training for Trouble
Boston, USA

'You can't expect consistent behaviour from a dog if you don't treat the dog consistently'

The strength of the bond between Asa, a small black-and-tan German shepherd, and her police handler, Troy Casey, was obvious. As Troy scratched the top of her head Asa sat leaning into his legs, looking up expectantly, waiting for the next command.

The Boston Police K-9 Training Center trains dogs in explosives and drug detection, as well as in searching and apprehending criminals. 'We purchase dogs between a year or a year and a half old,' Troy told me. 'There are specific vendors who import dogs and deal with a number of police departments. Buying the dogs at that age means we can get right to work with the training. If you have a breeding programme, you're taking a gamble on how the dog's gonna turn out. When they're a year old, we can test the dogs to see if they have the right character foundation that we need to train them. All dogs are checked for physical faults that may not be diagnosed until the dog is several months old. If we run into any issues during training, then we can always replace that dog with another from the vendor.'

The successful dogs have a strong hunting drive and a willingness to work with a handler. Each dog has to have the right temperament, so that if it's called on to work on patrol or for detection it has confidence in all environments. One officer praised the German shepherd in particular for its keen sense of smell and hearing, its agility, loyalty and obedience. 'You can't beat that – you really can't.' All these aspects of a dog can usually be assessed reasonably early, but it's not until they're older that they exhibit the right defensive behaviour, based on fight not flight instinct.

The dog and handler take a fourteen-week training course together. The handler has to have confidence in the dog, know what his dog is capable of and know how to use him on the street. When they come across situations they haven't met in training, trainer and dog need to understand what's happening and be able to respond quickly and correctly. Nothing can replace a dog trained in this work, but at the same time the handler has to keep in mind that his partner isn't a machine but a living thing that, in certain situations, can make mistakes. The handler has to be careful not to give his dog a task that he'll fail. Most importantly, he has to trust his dog.

After they've completed the initial training course, the dogs are trained twice a month for the rest of their working life. With time and training, different commands focus the dog on different tasks; his attitude changes depending on the focus. He needs to be calm and to ignore other people if he's going into a house to look for drugs, for instance, but he has to be fired up to chase a suspect.

Using a colleague's dog, Troy demonstrated how the animals are trained to negotiate a formidable obstacle course designed to give them confidence and to get them used to the various obstacles they'll encounter when working on the street. 'In the initial training, the handler does everything alongside his canine partner so the dog has no hesitation about jumping into widows, on to platforms, or into tight crawl spaces in an attic. Most of our training is reward-based and handler-based, so a nice bond is created between the dog and the handler. If we forced them to do things through compulsion, the dogs wouldn't be as reliable as they are when they enjoy working with the handler.' As the German shepherd went round the obstacle course, jumping hurdles, going through a fake window, up and over a vertical wall, through the window of a car door, over ramps, under low platforms and through a long pipe, his handler was there every step of the way, encouraging him, making sure he completed every task and rewarding him with praise and a treat at the end.

Then he ran up and bit me on the ankle (the dog, not the trainer). That was the first time I'd been bitten by a big dog since Slammie and Hushie attacked me as a child. Excitement had got the better of this one and he let go immediately, but he had proved my point: I don't get

257

on with foreign dogs, nor they with me. Fortunately no damage was done.

Troy then demonstrated a 'box search', used to train a dog to search buildings by sniffing cracks at the bottom of doors to locate a suspect. Six large boxes, one of them containing Troy's colleague, were arranged in an enclosure. Asa, Troy's own dog, had to decide which was the right one.

'Boston Police K-9! Come out! Boston Police K-9! I'm going to loose my dog.' Then, removing Asa's lead. 'Find him!'

Asa made her way round each of the boxes until she reached the last one. She sniffed at the door, moved away, then returned to sniff again before barking to alert her handler that she'd found something.

Putting her back on the lead, Troy yelled, 'Boston Police! Come out of that box!'

As Scott emerged, hands in the air, Asa strained towards him, barking, her teeth audibly slamming shut, until a sharp command from Troy had her almost bouncing back into a sit beside him. The dog's only job is to find people; its barking frightens them into submission.

When I took Arthur to puppy classes jumping up was out of order, yet Asa was jumping up on Troy. Different rules for different dogs? 'You don't want a house pet greeting people by jumping up on them, but for the police dogs it can be a form of reward. I allow her to do it, but she also knows that at certain times she's not gonna do it. If I'm going out to dinner and I go out to put her in her kennel, I don't want her jumping up on me. So it's allowed when I'm in uniform but not if I've got different clothes on.' Although a family pet, Asa prefers to sleep in the kennel outdoors, only using her crate indoors when the weather's too hot or too cold to stay outside.

I didn't understand why someone who so obviously cared about his dog would give it a kennel. I wouldn't dream of keeping a dog outside. It's a bit like having a TV and keeping it in the yard. I've chosen to share my life with dogs, so they share my house with me. It's true that I share my life with horses and they're kept in a stable, but they're impractical in the house. Although Jean once suggested keeping Arthur and Tina in a run outside, leaving the house to Mary, I wouldn't have the heart to separate them from us like that. Perhaps if I had a German shepherd, I'd feel differently. I know a couple of them quite well, and they're not dogs that get my pheromones going in quite the way others do.

Among the familiar commands in English, I noticed that Troy also used German commands. He explained that a lot of officers used German – they can't be confused with anything anyone else says, and they're mostly sharp, one-syllable words that catch the dog's attention immediately.

Another exercise in control was the recall. The handler has to be able to recall his dog by voice command in case the suspect takes off across a busy two-lane highway or if an innocent person steps out of their house or out of their car and gets between the dog and the suspect. The dog has to stop on command reliably even when he's psyched up.

Officer David Miller had his dog Rex in the back of his car, primed and ready to go. The car stopped, lights flashing, as Dave stopped his suspect (aka Officer O'Brien). 'Let me talk to you for a second. Put your hands up for me. . . .' As soon as the 'suspect' fought back, Dave pressed a button on his belt so that the back door of the car swung open for Rex to come to his aid. As Rex caught up with the 'suspect' he sank his teeth into his specially padded sleeve, not letting go until he was called. Immediately he returned to his trainer's side, even though still fired up, barking and baring his teeth.

Having a sixty-pound dog hanging off your arm can inflict some serious damage but, as Dave said, that's the price you pay for not stopping when the police tell you to. The more aggressively the victim resists the dog, the more fiercely the dog clings on. It was an extreme version of the game I'd seen the wolf cubs playing in Yellowstone, fighting over a scrap of pelt, or of the tug-of-war game with a toy with which Troy rewarded Asa.

Within moments, the 'suspect' was under arrest. Rex's concentration remained fixed on Dave the whole time. He was only interested in the fact that someone had pushed his partner. Despite the nature of these training sessions, with the handlers taking the role of suspect, all the handlers and their dogs get on. After each dog has been rewarded for his swift actions, everyone forgives and forgets and carries on working together, often in teams.

Explosives detection dogs such as Betty, a young black labrador belonging to Officer Langa, can also be trained to find firearms that have been used in crimes. What the dog looks for is the smokeless powder consistent with firearms. Kept on a long lead, Betty made her way round the sides of the building with her nose practically glued to the ground. Her handler constantly encouraged her and told her to 'Seek.' After finding nothing around the house or on the windowsills, her attention turned away to the path and beyond. Suddenly she smelled the powder, ran up a short incline and sat down. She had found the spot where Troy had hidden the gun under a pile of dead leaves and snow.

Just like the search-and-rescue dogs in Yellowstone, these dogs live with their trainers at home from the moment they're acquired. Betty has lived with Officer Langa and his young family since October 2007 and has been an unqualified success as a family dog. She's been spayed because that's a requirement of the working dog – no distractions. 'She's very quiet. She doesn't bark, she doesn't scratch – all she does is sniff.' Betty's a food reward dog, so the only time she eats is when she finds something. She never has a bowl of food put in front of her, so even when Officer Langa is off duty he still sets up different kinds of explosive in safe amounts around the house. If she finds it, she gets hand-fed. That's what keeps her drive going. Once again, this was an example of natural instincts harnessed through positive reinforcement. The dogs' working life usually lasts until they're about nine or ten years old. Pensioned off, they live out the rest of their days with their handler.

The majority of the work carried out by this K-9 unit involves building searches and narcotics. If someone breaks into a building, a dog and its handler are called rather than a group of police officers. The dog knows whether there's a person in the building the moment it goes through the door. The handler has to watch the body language of his dog. Are his ears pricked up? Is he moving quickly or slowly? Are his movements smooth or jerky? Is his tail wagging? Having trained with the animal, the handler can interpret the answers his dog's giving. Another of the officers explained how the canine officers tend to work on their own or with another canine officer. 'When I go in with my dog, I'm very confident he's gonna find the person and that he's gonna protect me and himself.' In training, everything is thrown at the dogs. They are put in every situation and the handlers may even throw a kick or a punch at them. 'Nothing hard enough to break a rib but to see what the dog will take, what he's fearful of. If you raise a hand or a foot and the dog shies away, they're no use to us.'

When the drug unit's at work they will respond to a call from the public, pull over a vehicle belonging to someone they've been investigating or enter a house that's been under surveillance. This team's primary concern is to find the dealers themselves. By the time the dog arrives, the suspects are usually sitting in the house handcuffed, under arrest. The dog's job is to find out where the drugs are stashed. People dealing large quantities hide them pretty well.

These dogs are super-obedient. They respond to the love of their handler and the way in which work is made fun. Once again, I was impressed by how the skill of a trained police dog in the modern world depends on the dog's acceptance of its handler as pack leader, the bond between the two of them and the enjoyment the dog takes in his work.

Back home with our own less than super-obedient dogs, while I was away Philippa had successfully contacted Sarah Fisher. A week or so after I got back Sarah turned up with a friend called Tina, though she didn't bite anyone. In the meantime we'd seen Sarah on *The One Show* successfully using her TTouch method to calm a stressed-out pony, so we'd been given some hope.

What was great was that Tina the dog actually attacked Mary in their presence. It's always hard, I think, for people to believe that this pretty, needy little thing with big brown eyes and an insatiable need to be stroked is actually really vicious. We had shut Arthur away in another part of the garden as we showed Sarah our other two dogs outside. She started by working with Mary, showing us TTouch. The circular movements of the fingers and hands all over the body activate the function of the cells and awaken what they call cellular intelligence. It's done on the entire body, and each circular TTouch is complete within itself. It isn't necessary to understand the anatomy of the animal to be successful in speeding up the healing of injuries or ailments, or changing undesirable habits or behaviour. Sarah went on to give Tina the dog some clicker training, rewarding any good behaviour such as sitting with a click and a reward. But, as she took her attention away from Tina for a moment to explain to Philippa what she was doing, Tina launched an un-provoked attack on Mary.

Sarah gasped. 'That's nasty!' We separated them and put leads on both. Tina the dog loves attention of any kind, so a bit of circular movement kept her very happy while Sarah explained the way she saw things. She felt that because basic training had been missing in Tina's early puppyhood she hadn't learned to socialise prop-erly, but she also said that our problem wasn't as severe as we perhaps thought. Tina and Mary spit, snarl and snap at each other, but blood is seldom drawn. If they were really serious about it they would rip holes in each other. I must say that I found this hugely encouraging. We found the attacks so horrific, I guess, because of all the sweetness we anthropomorphically projected on to our little cuties.

Sarah also pointed out that Mary carried her little sausage tail tucked firmly down, which she said was a sort of cringe, and that this kind of over-submissive behaviour could well be what was provoking Tina. Mary, who doesn't usually take to the touch of strangers, seemed to like the little clockwise circles that Tina the lady was making in her fur. I've always found Tina the dog to be particularly attentive and biddable – apart from the attacking thing, that is. Both Sarah and Tina the lady spotted this, saying that she was a very bright little animal and that maybe she wasn't being taxed enough in her day and that this had caused a kind of delinquency in her. This was exacerbated by our temporary small living space, her lack of early training and the by now semi-established behaviour pattern. This seemed to me to make great sense. The most difficult thing about preventing the attacks was going to be, as we already knew, that we had to be on the ball all the time to stop every single one. Sarah was quite clear that you can't expect consistent behaviour from a dog if you don't treat the dog consistently.

The day after the TTouch visit I noticed Mary carrying her tail straight up and walking with a real skip in her step. Perhaps this method was going to be the answer. A couple of days later, Sarah wrote to us.

. . . Tina Audrey has definitely learnt to throw her weight around when it comes to interaction with Mary Elizabeth, but she has so much potential for change that I would hope that with time and patience she learns to have a little more self-control.

265

I missed her initial launch at Mary Elizabeth, but from watching her face and body posture following the scrap I would imagine that she does give a warning that she is about to embark on her bullying tactics, although obviously this may only give you a split second to intervene before she actually makes contact.

Although there was a lot of noise and Mary Elizabeth hurt her tooth I do think that there is more noise than actual physical contact at the moment. There would be serious bloodshed if she really meant business, but this does not mean that it will never escalate to serious levels if she continues to respond to Mary Elizabeth in this way . . . . I believe that Tina Audrey would benefit from some training. You can teach her a lot at home and include Emily in the exercises, but you will all need to be consistent in your approach otherwise she will get confused. Training classes are an excellent idea . . .

Tina Audrey needs to learn that she is to look to you both for guidance and direction. Whilst free play with Arthur Colin is fabulous and necessary, she does need to respond to you and your cues. If she is allowed to do as she pleases all the time she will do just that, which will continue to include launching herself at the peaceful Mary Elizabeth whenever it takes her fancy.

The fact that she is good around food is a HUGE bonus, and she is delightful with people and Arthur Colin, so there are some really good foundations here for some really positive results. . . . I get the feeling that Tina Audrey may have been allowed to harass Mary

Elizabeth from an early age and it has escalated from there. Rough play in puppyhood needs to be checked early, otherwise young dogs can become too big for their paws as they start to mature. This does not mean, though, that she is incapable of learning any new behaviours. Dogs learn and continue to learn throughout their life.

Do you think that it would be possible to lead-walk Mary Elizabeth and Tina Audrey together without the company of Arthur Colin? Even just around the garden, so that they learn to enjoy each other's company. Use food, physical contact and lots of praise when they are responding well. I appreciate that you are both busy, but even a few minutes each day should bring some positive results. Tina Audrey needs to learn that good fun is to be had with you both in Mary Elizabeth's company.

Set yourselves and Tina Audrey up for success by teaching her to sit and wait around doors and the garden gate. All the dogs can be taught this useful exercise, and once you have a solid structure you can afford to be more flexible in your approach.

Dogs love learning new skills. They enjoy being successful, just like humans, and a well-trained dog will carry those skills forward into all aspects of their lives, which includes interaction with other animals and people.

It was interesting watching Tina Audrey with Arthur Colin when we were out in the yard, as there were times when she became snappy with him during their playtime. The fact that Arthur Colin is bigger, is male, plays the same types of games and ignores her behaviour is probably why she does not treat him the same way.

The TTouches will help Mary Elizabeth to develop more confidence and will give you some positive tools that you can use to help reduce any feelings of guilt that you may have!

Sarah seemed not to think that she'd been involved too late in the day, which came as a huge relief. She also sent us a sheet of exercises that we could try ourselves at home. We began to devise ways to keep Tina entertained or distracted, getting her attention by calling her over or throwing a ball whenever we intercepted a bad look. We'd already arranged with Rosemary Young, whom I'd met at the Melplash puppy classes, to come up to the farm to help me train Arthur to a more advanced stage. Perhaps she would agree to do some work with Tina and Emily too. Training the dogs together would be fun for Emily and me. But before we were able to start that, I had other dogs to see. Other dogs that, far from being bone-idle like mine, were making themselves useful in a very special way.

18

Behaving Obediently

Buckinghamshire

'Once you've found the right dog, the only way to get them to perform those tasks, whatever they are, is to make it fun for them'

Standing on a large grassy lawn, I made my way along the line of assorted dogs and their handlers, trying to identify the different crossbreeds. First up was Kent, a large alert black dog with an obviously gentle temperament who looked like a retriever-cum-poodle but was in fact an Irish water spaniel/retriever cross. After him came Jasper, a big greyhound/labrador cross; then Vinny, a small perky brown dog who looked more like a Shih Tzu crossed with a saxophone brush than the Lhasa Apso/cocker that he was; Crocker, a curly grey-haired dog with a long tail, turned out to be a poodle/American cocker spaniel; Womble, an enthusiastic shaggy black-and-white dog of unknown origin, must have had a bit of bearded collie in him; Mallow, a frisky Yorkiepoo no less; Guinness, a black labrador/working cocker spaniel cross – my household in one dog! And finally black Qbert, a handsome labrador/golden retrie-ver cross, one of a litter of ten who all had names beginning with Q. I was quietly impressed with my success in the game, proving to myself that I was able to identify so many of the breeds.

But these friendly, waggy animals were far from being any old mutts out for a stroll. They were a typical selection of hearing dogs for the deaf. These can come in any shape or size from a Chihuahua to a standard poodle. What matters most of all is their health, their biddability and their enjoyment of human company.

The headquarters of the Hearing Dogs for Deaf People in Princes Risborough, Buckinghamshire, is an impressive modern complex of single-storey training houses, kennels and offices. The organisation was started in 1982, gradually taking on more dogs and staff to outgrow its former headquarters so that in 1999 they opened the first buildings on this site. In 2007 it placed Badger, its fourteen hundredth dog.

Several of the working dogs that I'd already met were examples of dogs traditionally bred for a purpose. Now I wanted to see what use new crossbreeds might have in the modern world. Having started me off with the guessing game, Chris Allen, the Puppy Socialising Manager, proposed to demonstrate how their tempera-ments can be ideally suited to this work. He explained that the dogs used by the charity arc usually unwanted and either donated or from welfare organisations and rescue centres.

'We supply them to people from all walks of life so we train small, medium and large dogs, all with different activity levels. We can match the dog to the right person. What you hope for is to get the best of both breeds. For instance, the spaniel in Crocker makes him adaptable and fond of hard work, while the poodle in him means he doesn't moult so he'd be good for someone with allergies or who worked in an office or school where there might be people with allergies. Guinness is such a lively, enthusiastic dog that he would suit someone constantly on the go. He'd work happily from whenever he wakes up to the moment his owner goes to sleep. He'd make a great family dog, but he'd be hopeless in a flat or with someone in their nineties.' Alternatively, if a deaf person already owns a dog, it can be trained here for a few months, as long as its temperament's suitable, and then returned home.

'Generally,' Chris explained, 'we socialise new dogs, have puppy classes for them and then train them before they're placed with a deaf person. We also have deaf people on site working with the dogs before they enter their new home.' If a potential owner is getting a dog for the first time, they can stay at the centre for a day or two to get a feel of things. After all, feeding the dog or taking him out for his last pee doesn't appeal to everyone. Chris pointed out the obvious pros and cons: 'They give companionship and security, and alert other people to their owner's hearing loss. But if you don't like dogs or are worried by them, then the dog will pick up on those signals and the working partnership may not flourish.'

Once the dog is trained and established in his new home, he and his owner will be checked on by someone from the charity once a year. If there's a problem the charity gives them extra support at home until the difficulty's ironed out, or it will take the dog back for a couple of weeks' refresher course.

The charity desperately needs more dogs to fulfil its two-year waiting list, but can only take on dogs that have the right temperament. The trainers have to guide that loyalty and eagerness to please in the right direction, so that the dogs can work reliably and consistently for a deaf person. The absence of Staffies, pit bulls and lurchers was no coincidence. 'When a person wants to communicate with a deaf person, they generally come very close so they can make good eye contact and lip-read,' Chris explained. 'If we used one of the guarding or more aggressive breeds, they might not allow anyone to enter the personal space of the deaf person. We don't want dogs to react to people by guarding their owner against them because that can isolate the owner more, especially in a work environment. We need dogs who like being stroked. Lurchers generally combine being too laid back around the home with too strong a chase instinct to make a good hearing dog.'

Listening to Chris reminded me of my mother, who had become hard of hearing late in her life, so I know how isolating deafness can be. She didn't get another dog after Jemima, but I often wished she had. She never saw dogs in the same light as I do, so certainly didn't regret not having one. None the less, I think a dog might have given her some companionship. They're funny, too. Having pride in a dog and being approached by people who want to ask about him is really gratifying.

We stayed outside for a short but impressive demonstration of basic training techniques. The trainers use British Sign Language as well as the voice, because some deaf people may have speech difficulties. A hand raised above the head and the dogs sat; a hand towards the floor and they lay down. 'All the training is done through positive reinforcement,' Chris explained. 'We use food or a toy, or we make a big fuss of them. It's really whatever motivates that particular dog. If we use food we take it out of their daily food ration, so they don't put on any weight.'

Now that Mary's getting on a bit she's going slightly deaf and so I've begun to try teaching her to respond to my own signs, although I can't think of anything more to do than wave her on! She either responds or she doesn't, depending on the mood she's in. I'd also hoped that signing might help me deal with her when she's with Tina. If I can signal silently, then Tina won't hear and won't know that I'm giving Mary attention. Rosemary had said she would teach me signals for Arthur too, to give me some extra control over him when we're out riding.

I was glad to go inside out of the cold to see the next stage of the training. Teal, a bright-eyed brown Nova Scotia duck-tolling retriever/springer spaniel cross (that's enough dog breeds!) with white paws, a white blaze and a whitish nose with feathered ears and tail, was going to demonstrate what he could do. He wore the official burgundy-coloured Hearing Dogs for Deaf People vest and trotted obediently at the heel of his trainer, Tim, as we went into one of the mock-up homes used for training.

The first job the dogs learn is how to respond to an alarm clock. In the twin-bedded room, Teal lay quietly on a white mat in a corner of the room while I got under one of the duvets and Tim set a kitchen timer by the side of the bed. As soon as the alarm went off, Teal leaped to his feet, raced across the room and jumped on the bed – not a million miles from Mary's morning pin-down – to be rewarded by a treat that I was holding under the duvet and a lot of fuss. Job done, he scampered out of the room towards the kitchen in search of breakfast, the usual reward Tim gives him at home. If he'd been a larger dog, he'd have been trained to sit on the floor by the bed and put both front paws up on it – better than squashing his owner to death.

We moved into the fairly spartan living room, where Teal could show us what he does when the phone rings. 'If we were training a dog for you, we'd need to know where your phone was and the sound it makes so that we could set up the same situation here,' Tim explained. 'Teal's a demonstration dog and used to working with up to eleven different sounds, but the dogs that come into the centres are trained to specific sounds in specific homes.'

A dog being taken into busy towns or a noisy work-place would need to be able to work to more sounds than a dog who spent most of his time at home. The important thing is to train them to distinguish between each sound. At a late stage in the training the trainer sets off a doorbell, a smoke alarm and so on when the dog is least expecting them. By being rewarded when they give the correct response, they start to recognise the difference between them.

A medium-sized dog like Teal has to be trained to respond with an alert signal, which must never be confused with him wanting to play or have a cuddle. He comes up to his owner, sits down and puts his front paws on him, keeping his bum on the floor. A larger dog would be trained only to use one paw to touch the owner on the leg, to avoid accidentally knocking him over. The dogs are trained to be persistent, running to the phone and then returning to the alert position as many times as necessary until their owner reacts.

After watching Tim show me exactly what was involved I sat in an armchair, making sure Teal knew that I had a treat in my hand. Excited by the thought of food, he jumped up, trying it on. But I stayed firm. Once he had his bum on the ground and his paws on my leg in the alert position, I rewarded him.

Tim stood behind me so that, if needed, he could help Teal touch me when the phone went off in case he was uncertain about working with me. At the first ring, Teal dashed over and adopted the alert position. One treat down. Of course, if I were deaf I wouldn't know which sound he was alerting me to. The door? The phone? The smoke alarm? My response had to be to ask him, 'What is it?' by opening my arms wide.

Immediately Teal led me to the side table on which stood the phone and a minicom which lets a deaf person type their conversation down the phone line. He was rewarded with a biscuit. Tim seemed a little miffed that Teal had worked better for me than he had for him in the demonstration, justifying it by saying, 'I think we sparked him up with that nicer piece of food.' And I thought we might have sparked him up by our obvious remarkably quick bonding – ah well.

For Teal, working with me was like being transferred from the trainer to a new owner. Naturally, having worked with one trainer for some time and now being expected to work with a stranger, he was bewildered at first. Normally it would take about a week for the new partnership to bond. The dog and its new owner would spend time together in one of the training houses, getting used to one another and working with the trainer to-wards a good handover.

The next demonstration was the smoke alarm. Teal was flat out on the carpet. Would he save my life or would he carry on snoozing? I called him over to give him another treat, reminding him that, if he played his cards right, there might be another where that one came from. As soon as the alarm went off Teal came over and sat in the alert position, front paws on my knee. Time for another treat before I stood up and, taking a step forward, spread my arms to ask, 'What is it?' Immediately he lay at my feet so that I couldn't walk any further.

This time, since the practice was over, I could play with Teal just to show that the training exercises are all good fun really. In the fake world of imitation homes, what Teal did looked quite straightforward. But the dedication and care of the trainers who effectively harness the dogs' vocabulary to serve our needs was impressive. These intelligent, friendly and perfectly trained dogs show what can be achieved with a dog who has the right temperament. Once you've found the right dog, the only way to get them to perform those tasks, whatever they are, is to make it fun for them.

19

Tails from the Green Room

Los Angeles and London

'They say never act with children or animals, but I'd never say don't act with a dog'

On the subject of working dogs, it would be hard to write off the dogs from my own profession. From Lassie and Rin-Tin-Tin to Toto in *The Wizard of Oz* and Eddie in *Frasier*, there's a long line of dog actors who have been just as entertaining as their human counterparts. They say never act with children or animals, but I'd never say don't act with a dog. Take the Jacques Tati films, for example – they're gorgeous because they're filled with dogs.

Perhaps the greatest dog screen legend I've met was Laddie, bred by Bob Weatherwax, son of the man who bred Pal, the first dog to play Lassie in the 1940s. Laddie's a ninth-generation descendant. The original Lassie became internationally famous after starring in *Lassie Come Home* and going on to become the fourth highest earner in the MGM studios at that time, with a tidy income of 268 million dollars.

The family sold the rights in the name and character of Lassie to a company which uses its own dogs. As a result, the latest of the dogs in the Weatherwax lineage has had to adopt the performing name of Laddie. I arrived in LA when he was filming a public service announcement and went along to meet him. A smart car with the number plate LASSIE pulled up and out he stepped: a handsome, long-coated, sable-and-white rough collie with a long thin nose and white blaze, a white collar and dark, soulful eyes. One Weatherwax dog after another has been bred to retain these distinctive markings. Bob brushed Laddie to look his best before folding over the tips of his ears and attaching a small weight with some gum to keep them in place. Before the filming one of the bits of gum got lost, so Laddie had the indignity of appearing with one ear up and one down. Now a retired nine-year-old, Laddie seemed less than happy at having been brought out to work, but then every star has his off day.

After filming had finished, Bob told me about his father who'd started the business. He'd obviously been a man who knew how to bring the best out of his dogs. 'There's a shot in *Lassie Come Home* where the dog comes in and knocks Liz Taylor down, then he goes back and shakes his head, remembering who she is. He lies down, puts his head down because he knows he's done a bad thing, then he crawls up and just nudges her, then he nudges her again. No director was telling my father to do that. He knew the timing, what the dog would do and how to really milk it and make everybody cry.' Bob learned the same skills from his father, who taught by example. 'He said, "Just keep your mouth shut and your eyes open and you may learn something. Just do as I say and figure it out later." That's how I learned.'

Despite their success, Bob maintains collies aren't the most adaptable dogs for studio work. Other breeds, such as golden retrievers and German shepherds, are better. They're not smarter, but they're more easily manipulated. 'There's a lot of things collies just don't want to do,' he explained. 'The reason why is because they were bred to sit up on a mountain with a shepherd and just guard the sheep. They're tough dogs and they'll fight. That's what they're meant for. They're bred to be suspicious, so I have to go through a lot of socialisation with them.'

I wondered whether their close working partnership meant that Bob has to forego the companionship that the rest of us look for in our dogs. He was quick to put me right. 'No. Matter of fact, he's very close to me. The closer I can keep him to me and the more he knows my voice inflections, the better I can get him to work. He lives in the house and sleeps in bed with me. Sometimes I've woken up and thought he was my ex-wife. . . .'

Wherever Bob and Laddie go, Throttle, a little terrier, goes too. If Laddie gets upset or spooked by anything, Throttle's there for canine companionship. When they were younger and making personal appearances, Laddie would perform a twenty-minute act involving Throttle as a comedy part.

Remembering all those movie greats from the dog world, I was sorry to hear Bob say that animatronics were taking over from the real thing. 'They'd better get some trainers and some movies that portray loving dogs. They don't make people just wanna bring the dog back in their life as they did after *Old Yeller* or *Lassie Come Home*. These days it's all comedy and done with computers and stuffed dogs. That's why I think people aren't into dogs as much as they used to be. It's just a different world now. They need somebody to come up and make another tearjerker classic with a dog to re-establish dogs' popularity. Doesn't matter what breed, does it?'

Despite his reservations, I have to admit that voicing the character of Kipper, a black-eared brown-and-white puppy, for the cartoons based on Mick Inkpen's magical children's books was great fun. Emily loved those films, but I don't think until this day she knows he was me. If she was ever tired or upset, she'd love a soothing bit of *Kipper*. I loved voicing him, partly because Emily was tiny and this was an introduction to children's literature for me, but also because Mick is such a particular writer. With his friends Tiger, a grey terrier, and Pig, whose nephew Arnold continuously sucks his thumb, Kipper inhabits a very kind world where simple problems are solved with kindness.

Mick knew exactly the voice he wanted for Kipper, although I wouldn't have been that squeaky by choice. My first attempt was much deeper – I had Mel Smith in mind. We worked for a long time until Mick was happy. Recording all eighty episodes, Chris Lang, who did all the other voices, and I had such a laugh just sitting together in the studio in front of a blank wall with two microphones.

Working with live animals has taught me that you have to cut your cloth to whatever behaviour they're going to offer on the day. Patience is a quality that anybody working with animals must have in spades. They take time, like some child actors. And sometimes, even then, things don't always go the way they're planned.

The wranglers, or people who supply working animals, are invariably women, who have to work with crews who are invariably male. The amount of eye-rolling that goes on while time ticks by as we wait for an animal to do what's required of it is considerable. The worst I've ever worked with was a squirrel. What a tosser. His name was Nutty and he'd worked on the Carling Black Label ads. He was meant to be a real pro. All he had to do in this episode was run along a branch and take a bit of ribbon from a twig. I say 'All'. . . . Every time he was let go, he just shot off in the opposite direction. The whole afternoon disappeared in getting one shot.

The greatest pro I've ever worked with has to be Gremlin, the shaggy greyish mutt who appeared regularly in *Doc Martin*, looking a lot shaggier once he'd been in make-up where he was gelled to within an inch of his life. He was a sweet-natured dog who followed the Doc around whenever he got the chance. Sadly for him, the Doc couldn't stand him. Despite Gremlin's attentions, the Doc never changed his mind and tried to kill him or get rid of him quite regularly, even going as far as throwing a stick over a cliff and telling him to 'Fetch.'

We knew immediately that Gremlin was the dog for the job when we were auditioning for the part. We weren't looking for a dog that size, but rather one that would love the Doc despite being hated in return. We had to see how all the hopefuls would respond to me. His audition piece was to let me drag him round the floor by his fur or his legs – he didn't mind which. Otherwise, he sat looking lovely and loving. He was head and shoulders better than the rest. So, he got the gig.

But of course we had problems, even with him. In one episode we shot a few dream sequences where the Doc was dreaming about Louise kissing him, then woke up to find Gremlin in her place. We tried everything to make him kiss me. My chin was smeared with first cheese, then ham and finally smoked mackerel. But some dogs lick and some don't. Gremlin didn't. In the end, we gave up and I grabbed him and gave him a good kiss instead.

Once we needed him to pop up unexpectedly on the back seat of the car for the Doc to spot him in the rear view mirror. To encourage him, the poor trainer was lying with her head out of shot in my lap, holding a piece of sausage, waggling it about and saying, 'Up, up, up.'

There are out-takes of me laughing my head off. The good old boy did the shot, though.

In the third series, he was given a story line of his own where he had a romance with a Yorkshire terrier – they'll stoop to anything, these actors – that the Doc subsequently ran over. To find the right Yorkie to play the part, we had to find the right stuffed one first and then come up with a live match. It has to be that way round for obvious reasons. In the story, a couple turned up with the Yorkie in a handbag. The idea was that Gremlin would try to mount the dog, but once the creature was shaken out of the handbag it had no idea what to do. The trainer had boasted that the Yorkie was a pro but it wouldn't answer to its name, sit or do anything asked of it. Gremlin hadn't a clue what to do in that instance either, maybe he was gay.

Gremlin was with the show from the start and we got great value from him. He'd walk in and out of rooms when asked, even jump through windows. I yelled at him an awful lot in the story, which I had to do silently. We would add the sound later – otherwise I'd never have got anything out of him. All those times when he appeared to be following the disgruntled Doc I was in fact desperately whistling for him to follow me.

Philippa was the producer of the series and would bring Mary to visit me on set. There are countless scenes where Mary is at the bottom of the screen, just out of the frame. She'd wander in and we'd just carry on playing the scene around her. If anyone got put off, we'd have to retake the scene. One year she got the opportunity to star alongside Gremlin, when a teenage girl had a crush on the Doc and turned up at his surgery. 'I thought we could go for a walk, and I've brought Mary,' she said. The camera panned down and there was Mary on a lead pulling away from her, confused by me scowling at her. She was rubbish.

We all loved Gremlin, but by the third series he was getting on a bit and was having trouble jumping in and out of the window. Worse for him was having to power up the hill to the Doc's cottage where, to cap it all, there were seven steep steps. We could see him labouring a bit, but that made two of us. He died at the end of 2007. It's sad to think he won't be turning up any more. It was always good to see him, even though we always knew the day would be problematic. We're going to have to cast another dog, so perhaps we should think of asking Graham Norton and Andrew Lloyd Rover to put on a TV show, *Search for a Star*.

That wasn't Mary's only TV appearance. Much more to her taste is appearing on chat shows. I love having her there, partly for company but also because she draws the heat from me so that I don't have to regurgitate the same old behind-the-scenes-filming stories. She's been on *Loose Women*, sitting on my knee behind the bar that constitutes the set. She got bored while I was banging on but just sat quietly, resting her chin on the bar. She looked so funny and fed up that the director devoted one camera entirely to her.

When she appeared on *This Morning* with Philip and Fern she took against one of the cameramen, sitting her ground and growling at him as he was tracking in, until I got her to concentrate on her performance. The set for the show was another bar, but this time Mary had her own stool. Yet again I was sounding off, oblivious to what she was doing, until an injured Philip Schofield pointed out that she was sitting with her back towards him, deliberately blanking him. I guess she was holding out for *Parkinson*.

The next time we went on they'd made her a little sofa of her own, with a pile of cushions and a cake-stand containing a variety of foodies including some lamb chops that their chef had cooked for her. This time she was much more appreciative of Philip and sat gnawing on a chop throughout the interview. Cupboard love? There's nothing like it. Let's face it, she wouldn't have got that sort of treatment on *Parkinson*.

Tina hasn't aspired to being a TV star since she came of age on Paul O'Grady's show. She and Mary had just had their photograph taken by Lord Lichfield for the 2006 PDSA calendar. But Jean went mad when she saw the photo.

'Martin, Tina looks like a nightdress case. If you take that dog on TV looking as if she's been dragged through a hedge backwards, I'll sue you. So you'd better get your arse in gear – get down here and I'll trim her first.'

Jean is a force to be reckoned with, so I didn't dare say no. In due course we turned up at the show with Tina looking immaculate. To prevent his own dog taking an inappropriate interest in her, since she was in season, Paul presented her with a pair of pink frilly knickers. She did the sensible thing and ate them before French kissing Lizzie Maguire/Hilary Duff. Meanwhile Mary sat regally on my other side.

However well behaved the cockers appeared in public, we were still battling to improve the situation at home that, despite all our efforts, was getting much worse. The number of attacks was increasing, as was the intensity of the fighting. The constant vigilance and consistency needed to follow Sarah's method seemed impossible, given our busy lives. We always start off with such good intentions, but they gradually peter out as the demands of our lives get in the way. Nothing we do seems to teach this rather smart little dog not to fight.

None the less, we had kept up a combination of Cesar Millan's blocking techniques with Sarah's advice to channel Tina's energies into different activities. Rosemary had agreed that, when she came up to train Arthur and me, she would spend some time with Emily and Tina, reinforcing the basic commands but also showing Emily how to get Tina to dance with her and do tricks and some agility training. It would be fun for Emily and make use of Tina's intelligence.

On her first visit, we stood in the kitchen as I told Rosemary how many attacks there'd been that day. We'd ignored Tina, who had jumped up to greet her. I hate not making a fuss of the dogs – isn't that the best bit about having them? But Jean, Sarah and Rosemary had all advised that, if we wanted Tina to know her place in the family hierarchy, that's what we had to do. As we talked, Tina dashed next door and set on Mary who was asleep under the table. Three weeks later, Rosemary arrived to find Mary with blood on her ears and us almost at the end of our tether. Tina's teeth had pierced one of Mary's ears in the most ferocious fight yet. Emily and I took Rosemary into the garden to work with Arthur and Tina, but as soon as we'd stopped Tina rushed inside and attacked Mary again.

With forty years of experience under her belt, Rosemary's take on the situation was important to us. She thought the signs that this might happen must have been there when Tina was a young dog but, like lots of dog owners, we hadn't recognised her behaviour as a potential problem. In retrospect, it's obvious that she was right. But at the time, we hadn't known any better. We had thought Mary would be enough to socialise Tina. We had obviously been wrong.

The way Rosemary saw it, Mary had been the spoiled and over-protected alpha bitch resentful at a new puppy taking all the attention. With its mother, a puppy learns that if it does something wrong it gets a quick nip and so it learns not to do it again. End of story. When that's done in front of humans, they react – as we had – and that can startle the dogs and intensify the fighting. Rosemary felt that some dogs, like Tina, are born to be top dog, but that she'd met her match in Mary who refused to give up her position without a fight. If she'd lain back and submitted as some dogs would, then Tina could have taken the role of top dog and everything would have been fine. But Mary had fought her corner from the word go.

Because of all these factors, Rosemary felt the situation was never going to go away. However much training we put in to sort the problem out, she wasn't convinced that it would be the solution. As far as she could see, the habit was now too ingrained. In her experience, once a hostile situation between two bitches had reached this stage, one of them would eventually go for the neck of the other. One long canine tooth could pierce the jugular vein and that would be fatal. The alternative she presented was that Mary, now an old dog, might have a heart attack from the stress she must constantly feel, always fearful of imminent attack. Rosemary's other concern was that, if Tina went on attacking Mary, her aggressive behaviour might escalate and she might eventually bite a visiting child. We were both stunned. This was not what we'd hoped to hear.

In her view, we had to face reality. If we were determined to keep both dogs, the only solution would be to get a baby gate and keep Mary at peace on one side with Tina and Arthur on the other. We should accept that they were never going to get on and let them lead completely separate lives, even to the extent of walking them separately. Training Tina was still a good thing to do to occupy her mind and make her more biddable, but we would never be able to trust her not to make an unprovoked attack again.

When we got Tina, we had imagined a happy family mêlée of dogs and horses and people that all got along. If we accepted what Rosemary said, this was never going to be. Perhaps there really was no magic wand that was going to make everything all right, yet none of us could bear the thought of Tina being anywhere else but at home with us. We couldn't have Mary being killed, yet the idea of waking up and wondering where Tina was was too awful, especially for Emily. We were going to have to make some hard decisions.

I had to go away for five more days of filming, during which we would have time to reflect on the situation and decide what to do.

20

The Darker Side of Love

Liverpool and London

'Despite the mess we've made along the way, dogs
have still done fantastically well out of us humans'

I s there a darker side to our obsession with dogs? Does our love sometimes tip over into something more harmful than beneficial? We frown on the idea of genetically engineering humans, but for some reason it's still all right to do it with dogs. Yet we've bred all sorts of problems into our dogs in our search of the perfect animal. When I talked to Bruce Fogle in Tring, he had explained the problems that can arise from having a limited founder stock for a breed such as the Bernese mountain dog. He had gone on to tell me what happened to the King Charles spaniel. At the turn of the twentieth century an American, Mr Roswell Eldridge, offered prizes at Crufts to the breeders who successfully modified the shape of the King Charles spaniel to resemble the toy spaniel popular at the court of Charles II. So the Cavalier King Charles was born, its face more drawn out than the King Charles. The Cavalier is a pretty little dog and a perfect family companion, but it can suffer dreadful medical problems. Bruce explained that the founder effect was so dramatic that those early dogs which conformed to the new standard carried the potential for three problems in the dog today. 'The hind brain of forty per cent of Cavaliers prolapses, falling out on to the top of the spinal cord, which leads to a variety of conditions some of which are dreadfully serious and excruciatingly painful. Probably about fifty per cent of them have heart disease, and there's a high incidence of epilepsy.' Swedish breeders, however, have been successful in breeding selectively to postpone the onset of heart disease, extending the dogs' life expectancy. Other breeds have had their faces shortened. They may look cuter – or more ugly – but there's no doubt that they can suffer from eye and breathing problems as a result.

The inherent problem with creating any type of pedigree breed is that the breeder must beware the founder effect if there's only a limited gene pool. Bruce and I talked about all the new fashionable breed dogs: the labradoodle, the cockerpoo, the puggle and even the humble shitapoo. These are new crossbreeds being developed that have yet to be formally recognised by the Kennel Club. Might they develop their own problems? 'The first generation are almost invariably good healthy dogs, but if that evolves into creating a breed from a limited gene pool then we might be creating the same type of problem that we have with the Cavalier. I think it's great to cross-breed but I'm not that keen on creating a breed standard for that cross and creating a breed that has to conform to the breed standard that is shown at dog shows.'

There's no doubt that labradors are often affected by joint problems, and I wanted to know why. Arthur came with a sheet of instructions to prevent us putting his growing bones at risk of injury. We weren't to let him walk downstairs. What were we meant to do? Throw him out of the window? Walks were to be kept short until he was fully grown. I worry even now that we might be over-exercising him, but he so wants to come out with us when we ride. Like all labs, he loves exercise. When he had his knackers off, we were told to keep him quiet and only walk him on the lead. Before we knew it, he'd jumped a five-bar gate. He's so spiffy and fit that I think he's all right, but of course we won't know until later in his life.

Apart from harming the species with our dodgy ideas about breed purity, our over-indulgence of our pets – albeit with the best possible motives – is responsible for some long-term damage too. I visited the Royal Canin Animal Weight Management Clinic at the University of Liverpool to see where our relationship with our pets has come slightly unstuck. Here are vets who put owners and dogs on a diet course. Only the dogs have to stop eating, not the owners. Would I find that the 9 p.m. Shmacko routine, when Mary, Tina and Arthur get their evening treat, was doing more harm than good?

The first dog I met in the clinic was Rebecca, a beautiful brown lab with a coat like an otter. She was from working stock, so shorter in the leg than Arthur. She'd been referred to the clinic because her owner had reached an impasse. If they reduced the amount she ate any more, they'd start to harm her. She'd been the runt of her litter, 'the cutest but the weakest', and her arthritis had appeared early. While her owners worked, she'd been left with a loving dog-sitter who bought her whole cakes and massively overfed her. Her weight now put so much pressure on her joints that it was painful for her to move. She'd been on a diet, but her inability to exercise meant she'd stopped losing the pounds.

The dietician explained that to maintain muscle it was important to find the right diet and form of exercise. She thought that exercising in water, which would put no weight on the joints, would be part of the answer. Obesity causes a number of problems to joints, she explained, but body fat produces chemicals that can inflame parts of the body. Overweight dogs are more likely to become diabetic as well as to contract urinary and respiratory problems. The vet was convinced that obesity only occurs in domesticated dogs. The problem is often that, because they live with their dog day in day out, an owner doesn't notice the animal gradually putting on weight. Often, when it's pointed out, the damage has been done. We are responsible for creating this problem, and it's getting worse in both dogs and humans. There seems to be strong parallels between the two species.

After her owner had completed a thorough questionnaire and Rebecca had been examined, her blood pressure was taken before she was sedated. Because the Dexascan is a scanner originally intended for humans, the dog has to be laid on its back so that the software works appropriately. As she was carefully balanced to lie straight, she moaned quietly in her sleep. From the images produced by the scan, the experts could see that she had thirty-eight per cent body fat when the most she should have had was between thirty and thirty-five per cent. She needed to lose five kilograms to redress the balance. After four or five months of a special high-fibre diet, hydrotherapy and exercise programme, she would be rescanned to check her progress.

The precision of the treatment amazed me. The detailed information given by the owner, combined with the expertise of the clinical staff, surely meant that Rebecca was looking forward to a better, more energetic quality of life very soon.

Roxy was a super-friendly brown lab who had returned for a check-up after keyhole surgery on her arthritic elbow. The consultant explained that dogs usually start to develop these sort of conditions when they're six or seven months old. 'The biggest risk factor is genetics, but it's such a complex genetic trait that it's very difficult for breeders to know whether or not their dogs have it.'

Roxy, like Mary, was the only one in her litter to have such a problem. 'Environmental factors such as over-exercise or growing too quickly might bring out the disease, but genetics are by far the most important risk factor.' Nobody really knows why labradors are particularly prone to arthritis, unless perhaps their joints are looser because they were bred for swimming and re-trieving. They were known originally as the St John's dog, and every Newfoundland fishing boat would have one on board to retrieve fish and to pull in the fishing lines. They were first brought over to Britain in the early nineteenth century, and their retrieving abilities chan-nelled into making them excellent gundogs. They were recognised by the UK Kennel Club in 1903.

Six weeks after surgery, Roxy seemed very perky but was still limping. We went down to the Gait Analysis Lab where I walked her up and down a runway that measured the forces she put through her limbs. At the same time, reflective markers on her limbs translated to a digitial image showing how she used her joints as she moved. The sophistication of the monitoring machinery was fantastic and aided Roxy's diagnosis in a way that would have been impossible twenty years ago.

Oscar was a sweet four-year-old black-and-white spaniel with a full tail. When we met he was woozy from a pre-med prior to a hip replacement. Hip dys-plasia had led to arthritis, just as we'd been warned might happen to Mary. Like her, he'd just got unlucky. His X-ray showed the dislocation of the hip joint. Scrubbing up, I thought I might be too squeamish to watch the op. The whole thing was extra loaded for me because the patient was a little cocker. The theatre was like any human operating theatre, equipped with a lot of machinery and a slightly distressing 'Get-it-from-B&Q'

Makita hand drill for making a hole the same size as the ball they're inserting in the hip joint. All you could see of Oscar under the green sterile sheets was his little dry nose breathing in oxygen. It looked pretty barbaric as they cut through to the hip, but because Oscar was hidden I pretended his leg was just a piece of meat. The rasping sound as they cut through bone was quite disturbing all the same, but at least I wasn't sick and I didn't faint. An hour and a half later, the new ball had been attached to the thigh bone and the socket repaired. Once they'd closed up the flesh and stapled it together, it looked like a dog's leg again.

I found it quite moving that all these people and all this expertise were being used to stop a dog's leg hurting. Surely that's humanity working at a higher level.

I met up with Oscar later in the Recovery Suite. He lay quietly, happy to be stroked as he came round. Although spaniels are prone to problems with their hips and knees, as I knew too well, they often do very well after surgery provided they're kept confined for the first eight weeks or so. Oscar's future was bright.

I tried to pin down the consultant on whether or not dogs develop particular complaints that are directly down to our genetic tinkering with them. In Liverpool, they've done work comparing labradors to greyhounds. Labradors, as I mentioned, were only developed in the nineteenth century, whereas greyhounds are much closer to the proto-dog and have a history going back thousands of years. They are the only dog mentioned in the Bible. Research so far has found that greyhounds rarely get hip dysplasia, elbow problems or ruptured ligaments in the knee.

In Liverpool, they are researching and developing new treatments all the time. They've found that labradors are the most common breed with weight problems, and suspect some genetic link. The consultant explained, 'We need enough dogs to be able to look at the problem and to find out which genes may be involved. That means we could potentially intervene in a different way through a special breeding programme to try to minimise the problem to benefit dogs in the future.'

Should we try to breed genetic faults out of dogs? I don't know. I certainly don't know how you'd enforce something like that. What we like about a dog is what they do naturally as well as the special relationship we have with them. Breeding perfect breeds seems unimportant. The dogs that I saw at the clinic represented some of the damage inherent in some breeds thanks to our interference with them. If it wasn't for our love of dogs they'd never be in this mess in the first place, but at least we're trying to put it right. But I couldn't help thinking about the dog-sitter who spoilt Rebecca with cake. Too much love can be a dangerous thing. On the other hand, as long as you're not harming your dog you can't indulge your dog too much, in my book. Despite the mess we've made along the way, dogs have still done fantastically well out of us humans.

To see the extremes to which our passion for dogs can drive us, I took Arthur and Tina along to visit the Mutz Nutz Pet Boutique in London's Notting Hill. This is a cornucopia of every kind of dog accessory and toy you could dream of and many you couldn't. Perhaps the weirdest was the bride and groom outfits, although as someone who dresses up their dogs in Santa outfits on Christmas Day I can't really comment. Mutz Nutz have a Doggy Santa every Christmas with Jazz, who belongs to the owner, Jane Cooper, as Santa's little helper. 'I thought it was so bizarre the first time we did it, and now I just do it every year,' she laughed.

I found birthday party kits, IQ tests, Design Your Own Dog Collar kits, Bake Your Own Cookie kits and jewelled collars. Additive-free doggy treats, venison ears, pigs' ears and cows' ears – three per pack from those three-eared animals – crowded the shelves, and over the road there was even a dogs' deli where the customer can taste before buying. Arthur soon found a football, while Tina tried on a flying jacket from a huge range of dog clothing. I bought new leads and toys that you can stuff with treats, in the hope that they'd exercise Tina's brain and take her mind off Mary and take Arthur's off the carpet that he'd chewed down to the underfelt off the skirting board that was under attack.

Across the road with the deli is the Mutz Nutz Doggy Day Spa. If you're coming up to town for the day you can drop your dog off to be pampered, walked and fed until you collect it. I asked Jane what she could do for Tina and Arthur.

'We'd give you a twenty-minute consultation to know exactly what you want done with your dog, so we give you all the options. We'd give you choice of natural shampoos for the labrador. We'd work out what skin type he had, whether he had flaky skin, itchy skin. We'd find out a little bit about him and he'd get the full works: eye clean, ear clean, pedicure, massage. We do Brush and Hugs. He'd obviously have a bath, blow dry and spritz, so he'd leave smelling beautiful. Obviously the cocker would need more of a trim, so we'd discuss which one. We normally cut to breed standard, but it's up to you. Basically, they just spend a whole day being pampered and walked and fed.'

For anyone who doesn't like putting their pet in kennels for a day and is worried about whether they'll be as spoiled as they are at home, here's a promise that they'll be spoiled better. How great is that?

I wondered whether Jane drew the line at anything. 'People do dye dogs and paint their nails, but we don't. And definitely no piercings. [Can you imagine a King Charles with a Prince Albert?!] We do try to accommodate everyone, but there's something slightly wrong about all that. You can do the kind of bizarre that doesn't harm them, like a Mohawk haircut, but when people ask for things that are too much we'd say no. I do believe that dogs should be dogs.'

Working here, Jane has seen the extremes of dog love. Some dogs are carried everywhere and their feet rarely touch the floor. Some are vegetarian. She's noticed that the more pampered a dog is, the worse behaved it is, because it's given no boundaries.

In my book, there couldn't be enough of this sort of shop, just as long as no one's kidding themselves that the dogs are the ultimate winners. The dogs don't care whether or not they're dressed up, provided their movement isn't restricted. Let's face it, this is nothing new. People have been dressing up their dogs for years. The Victorians were fond of comic sketches and photos of their pets dressed up and performing tricks and tasks that had nothing to do with their own lives but reflected the society of their owners. This was a period known for its proper behaviour and stiff upper lip, yet there they were mucking about dressing up dogs in nightdresses. The idea that we're taking away their dogness is something that we project on to them. They have no vanity. They're going to continue being dogs, with or without the beret. I think we should reserve our judgement for more important things.

A few clicks online and a whole other world of dog indulgences can be found. A Japanese company has produced Bowlingual, a machine that translates dogs' barks into human language so you can understand what your dog is trying to say. In Melbourne, Australia, My Dog Café offers 'one-hour doggie birthday parties, complete with party hats and pupachinos, birthday cakes and a separate menu featuring dishes such as braised beef cheek, oxtail ragout and slow-cooked lamb shanks (without onion, garlic, seasoning or cooked bones, of course, and certainly not from a can).' If you've got money to blow, designer dog collars come diamond-studded, in platinum, silver or gold. Buy a horoscope to check your pet's future, or simply treat them with special perfume and sweaters or bedding. It's a whole other world.

The dogs that are treated to such attention have come a long way from the working dogs that were rewarded with a kind word, a bone and a warm place to sleep. Some of the treatments on offer to pets might be judged as a step too far, but if they're giving the owners pleasure and not harming the dog – what's the problem?

21

The Day the Dogs Ran Free
Mkomazi, Tanzania

'What might have happened if the original wolves hadn't opted to live with man, if they'd turned their backs on us and walked away?'

*B*orn *Free*, starring Bill Travers and Virginia McKenna as George and Joy Adamson, was the first feature film I was ever taken to see. After that, I read the books *Born Free, Living Free* and *Forever Free*: the story of Elsa the lioness who was released into the wild by Joy and George Adamson. By a strange quirk of fate, the first and only feature film I ever directed, *Staggered*, featured Virginia McKenna on an Outer Hebridean beach being chased by a naked me. Poor thing. Unscarred by this, we remained great friends. Coincidentally, we were filming not far from where Gavin Maxwell lived and the setting of his *Ring of Bright Water*, the second film I saw.

My appetite for wildlife books and films was unabated until one in particular caught my eye. The TV natural history film of Solo, an African wild dog puppy, triggered something else in my nine-year-old imagination. I couldn't tear myself from the screen. Solo was the runt of her family, a little chubby painted dog who was always attacked by her siblings whenever she left the burrow. She refused to give in to them and followed the pack on a fifty-mile trek in search of food and water – an ordeal that almost cost her her life.

There were shots of the pack moving off, leaving behind this little podgy triangle who had run out of steam. At this point, the film-makers stepped in to rescue her. This was quite notable, because intervening with the subject is one thing documentary makers don't normally do. Having saved her life, they put her with a pair of wild dogs and their five pups; surprisingly she was accepted and restored to the wild. I became so engrossed in Solo's story that I even asked if I could get the book that Hugo van Lawick, the film-maker, had written about her.

Ever since, I have been intrigued by this independent breed. Of course, although the African hunting dogs belong to the canine family, they are not directly related to the domestic dog. But, given that the dogs we know and love have done so well out of their relationship with us, I wanted to see what might have happened if the original wolves hadn't opted to live with man. If they'd turned their backs on us and walked away. The African hunting dog is a breed that has never sold out, and I wanted to know why. Having seen wolves in the wild, I was keen to visit another dog species that has never developed a rapport with humans.

I met Tony Fitzjohn for the first time in 1997 when I travelled to Tanzania to help translocate an elephant called Nina from the Mount Meru Game Sanctuary to the Mkomazi Game Sanctuary in the north-east of Tanzania, by the Kenyan border. While we were moving her, she was drugged and being rolled around in the transporter. My task was to keep her trunk from twisting so that she wouldn't suffocate. She lay on her side with me crouched in the gap between her front legs and her jaw, hanging on to her trunk. I made the most of my moment in Tanzania, lifting up her huge ear and having a good old sniff. I caught a muggy, musty smell, nothing like dog.

In 1989, Tony was given a mandate by the Tanzanian government to re-create Mkomazi, thirteen hundred acres of wilderness which had once been a wildlife refuge. For the previous eighteen years he had worked with George Adamson and the lions in Kora, five hundred square miles of thorn bush between Kenya and Somalia. Adamson was one of the original Kenya game wardens. In 1956, towards the end of his time in the Game Department, he was called to shoot a man-eating lion. The lion turned out to be a lioness and her three cubs. He rescued the cubs and was allowed to keep the runt of the litter – Elsa, whom he and his wife eventually released into the wild. After Elsa's death in 1961, George and Joy recaptured her troublesome three cubs and released them into the Serengeti. Following his retirement that year he devoted the rest of his life to his work with lions.

Tony joined Adamson in 1971 as a drifter with a dream. Together, they followed the progress of the lions and leopards they rehabilitated, collared and released, re-establishing them in the wild and studying their behaviour. The two men were constantly under threat from armed poaching gangs, not to mention the animals themselves. Trying to bring in four young lions for the night, Tony was savaged by one of them, surviving a near-fatal bite to his throat. Less than a year after Tony left Kora, Adamson was murdered by Somalian bandits when he went to the rescue of his assistant and a young European tourist in the Kora National Park.

Tony created Mkomazi out of the dust, building an infrastructure of roads, airfields and water sources, recruiting and training rangers and conducting an anti-poaching programme. In 1989, he created Tanzania's first rhino sanctuary. Down that scruffy airstrip they landed a Russian Antonov An-225, the largest plane in the world, with four rhino aboard. Subsequently, in 1995, he set up a breeding initiative for the endangered African hunting dog.

I flew into Mkomazi over the red earth roads and an occasional landing strip cutting through the bush, unusually lush and green for the time of year. Tony met me and flew me in his single-prop to the camp. I remembered how red it was when I first visited, but now, in a different season, there was every shade of green imaginable. Close by was the distinctive line of the Kenya–Tanzania boundary. 'This is perfect dog country,' Tony explained, 'with enough space to give them a pretty good chance of survival.' As we approached I could see two holding *boma*s, or enclosures, one on either side of a little rock promontory. Sangito, the head dog keeper, and Freddie, one of his helpers, camp here for weeks at a time, looking after the dogs.

Although these beautiful animals have a similar pack structure to wolves, there is one crucial difference. If the alpha male dies, his role is taken by his son. The dogs never accept a surrogate leader from outside the pack structure and that is why, unlike the wolves, they have never fitted in with man. Unfortunately, African hunting dogs are now on the verge of extinction, with fewer than three thousand of them in existence compared to the two hundred thousand at the beginning of the twentieth century.

When colonial settlers came to this part of Africa, they didn't like the way the wild dogs disembowelled their living prey and soon classified them as vermin. The first job of every game warden in those days was to go out and kill wild dogs. That view was passed on to the indigenous population, and the dogs gradually acquired a dreadful reputation that they didn't deserve. They've never been known to harm a human being. The price they've paid for their independence has been near extinction, and there are less than three thousand left in the wild. Now attitudes are changing towards them, but attitudes always change too late.

A man named David Anstey had originally set up the Mkomazi reserve in 1951. In an article he wrote in the mid-1950s, he said that there were far too many dogs here. 'What he meant by far too many, I don't know,' said Tony. 'Hundreds? They must have been following the elephant, the buffalo and the rhino. When I came here, I wasn't aware of the plight of the wild dogs. They used to come through Kora twice a year. I got to know them, could walk among them and thought how very nice they were, but as a lion and leopard man I didn't want dogs. But the more I found out about them, the more I thought I needed to do something and began researching. These were the animals that needed the most help round here. Then I got a letter from a Maasai elder on the Maasai Steppe telling me that the dogs were killing their sheep and goats, and were about to be poisoned. I needed no encouragement. I shot over there with Giles Thornton, who was in charge of field work.'

Rather than darting and drugging the adults, they decided to wait until the adults were out hunting and then raid the dens where the dogs had burrowed underground to have their pups. Over a week they conducted three raids, and lifted twenty-five pups that were about a month old. The Maasai agreed to keep in their stock for twenty-four hours on each occasion, during which the adult dogs were frantic. However, as Tony had hoped, after a day spent looking for their pups the dogs moved south of the Steppe and three weeks later were seen mating again. Having air-lifted the pups home, Tony had the makings of a founder population.

'I brought others in to help us, including Aart Visee, once vet at Rotterdam Zoo, who established a vaccination programme. I thought it would be easy, but it took us ten years to get right. Once one of them gets a disease they're all done for, because they greet each other by licking the face and anal end. They survived millions of years until we introduced diseases that have wiped them out.' After he'd successfully bred from the original pups, doubling their numbers and introducing a small number to the wild, a virulent strain of canine distemper wiped out forty-nine. The dogs had, however, all been vaccinated against distemper, so further research had to be carried out on the vaccination programme until it was fully effective.

I'd been here when the first puppies were introduced to the four large enclosures, so it was thrilling to arrive back on the day when Tony was releasing a new pack into the wild. I was introduced to the male dogs in their enclosure. They look nothing like their far distant relative, the wolf. Their distinctive multi-coloured coat in splotches of black, white, red, tan and cream is uniquely patterned on each dog and has earned them their scientific name *Lycaon pictus*, or painted wolf. They have broader, shorter snouts than the wolf, with a black muzzle, a daunting set of jagged teeth and large rounded pricked ears. Their distinctive, white-tipped tail looks like a fly switch. They have lithe, strong-looking bodies with muscular necks, deep chests and long thin legs. These are animals built for endurance.

Outside the *boma*s, a single female dog roamed quietly. 'She must be about seven now,' said Tony.

'She's not one of the original dogs, but from the ones we started with after the canine distemper die-off. It's a sad story. We released her with another female who was always a bit weird. The first night a leopard mauled the wonky one. We treated her and they set off again. The third night, the leopard came down and bit half the wonky one's face off so I had to put her down. This one was left on her own. We released her anyway, but when we brought in these other dogs she just stayed.'

Before releasing the seven dogs this time, two of them had to be radio-collared. Sangito had isolated two of the males in a small cage. They were frantic, biting at the frame and scratching at the earth. 'They don't like being cooped up like this,' Tony said, 'but they feel happier if they've got a buddy with them. I use the blowpipe to inoculate them against rabies and distemper, so they get a bit tense when they see it.' He crouched down, waiting until the dog he was collaring was in the right position before he blew. Within a couple of minutes, the dog's legs were beginning to give way, and within four he was out cold. 'It's a long way from the lions that George and I handled. We made sure it was the heat of the day and they were quite full, then we'd just talk to them as we fitted the collars – big collars with nuts and bolts. That was such a lovely, purist way of doing things, but we have to do this with these dogs.'

I followed Sangito as he carried the unconscious dog into the open, where he put him on the ground so that he could fit the sturdy collar. 'We fit them snugly, because the dogs swell up a bit when they're drugged and when they're released they'll be lean again. Each collar has its own frequency and will last between six to ten months before the batteries begin to fail and the stitching starts to go. They'll have dumped them before the year is up.' Although Tony's team is on top of the veterinary programme, they are still experimenting with batteries. This time they were using bigger ones than they had before in the hope of getting a better range. 'I think there'll be a fifty to sixty per cent survival rate, but we need to keep tabs on it. Being on the international border is difficult, but we're looking into the possibility of having someone on the other side covering them after release as well.'

We left the dog lying in the shade; after forty minutes or so Tony would give it the antidote. Meanwhile we crossed to a second enclosure, where one of two female dogs was to be put through the same procedure.

This would be the fourth pack from the programme to be released into the wild. Last time, Tony mixed the females and males in the enclosure before the release. This time he was racking up the sexual tension by keeping the sexes separate and trusting they would join up in the wild after being released separately too. 'In an ideal world I'd release them ten miles away and they'd all romp around the bush, meet up and have puppies, but here I'm playing a titillation game. They've got each other's scent and they can hear each other, so we'll see what happens.'

While in the programme, the dogs are covered for rabies with three shots in the first year. Erasmus University in Rotterdam isolated the canine distemper virus that destroyed so many dogs before, so now, for the first time, Tony's animals are covered with a new, specially produced drug from Merrill. 'I think distemper is responsible for a lot of deaths,' he said. 'People say that these dogs have suddenly disappeared from an area without trace and no sign of vultures. We found out that, when they get canine distemper, they become very sensitive to light and so they immediately went into their burrows. All we can do is hope these ones survive and stay out of trouble. So far we haven't had a problem except with this old lady.' He nodded towards the loose female. 'I think, when she links up with this lot, she might have a bit of a chance. Apart from her, the packs have been completely self-sufficient and made a kill on the second night. A lion is the dogs' big enemy, but if they hear one they become very alert and tend to stay away. The third worry is people, but there's not much we can do about that either.'

While he talked, he used the blowpipe to dart one of the females before she was brought from the timber and mesh cage to be collared. The one left behind started making twittering sounds of distress. 'The third female died just the other day,' Tony explained, 'and now someone's taken this one away. You hear them calling to each other like this in the bush when they've been separated after a big hunt, although I'm sure a lot of telepathic communication goes on too that we can't read.'

We left her in peace to conk out and returned to the first dog, where I was shown how to inject 1.2ml of Antisedan into the muscle in his rump. I stroked his coarse coat, grabbing my opportunity to sniff behind his ear – a good smell: musky, dusty but not like a dog – before I picked him up by the scruff of his neck and hind legs to carry him back into the open. I laid him under a low thatched shelter and stepped back to watch him recover while Sangito let in the rest of the pack.

'They're pack animals and their social hierarchy is all-important,' Tony explained. 'We can't put dogs back into the wild alone because they won't break away to join another pack as out-breeders. Females are normally the out-breeders, because only the alpha females are allowed to breed within the pack. If the beta breeds, the pups are usually killed – although on rare occasions they have been adopted by the alpha. That has led to the theory that it's not always infanticide, but that the pups are killed by the alpha trying to mix them with her own pups. The non-breeding females never break away until they've helped raise one group of pups. When they do break away, they never cross-breed with a domestic dog. That seems to be terribly important to their social system. It's amazing how well behaved they are in a pack. I'm told they're much tighter that a wolf pack. In the wild they'll go for antelope, impala, dik-dik, lesser kudu, lizards, anything like that. And they're the only meat-eating species that allow their young to eat first.

'Although they've never been domesticated by man, they don't mind us. They're nomads and all they want is their freedom. One thing they hate is denning – that's when they have to dig a hole, or den, in which to have their pups. They have to hang out there, lactating and then going off and returning to regurgitate food for the pups, when all they want to do is run. Before we got our first lot, Giles watched three packs on the Maasai Steppe: two in ant-bear holes and one in a cave on the hillside. After about four and a half weeks, the females couldn't bear it any longer and had to go hunting. None of them stayed behind with the pups, who were savvy enough to hide if danger came. That's when Giles moved in with three Maasai men and four Durobos to lift the pups. While they were digging out one of the holes, a female arrived home. They don't bark, but she made a typical cough. One of the Durobos took a burning brand from the fire and threw it in her direction, so she took off. But she knew what was going on.'

While he talked, we watched the dog coming round. He was soon sufficiently conscious to want to join the others. As he regained the use of his legs they stood around him, making their curious squeaking noises and comforting him.

Then we went to look round the other three compounds that contained the two parent dogs, both about seven or eight years old – an age well beyond the four or five years they could have expected in the wild – and belonging to the third generation. 'We're going to have to keep the old boys, because we'd be turning them out to their death now. But they're quite happy here. They remind me of those old boys in African villages who sit around under a tree and bullshit all day.' We would be releasing the second generation the next day when the drugs would have passed through the systems of the two collared dogs. As we walked around the dogs took no notice of us – although Tony started breaking small branches from the trees to show me how, after a while, the dogs would follow us to see what we'd been doing.

Despite being a lifelong cat man (big cats, I should stress), Tony has obviously become attached to these dogs. I wondered whether he would miss them when they were released or celebrate their freedom. 'Everything I do in my life involves a mixture of emotions. How happy can you be when your fingers are crossed for their survival the whole time? But yes, I'll be happy they're free. I've seen them from the plane streaming through the country like Alfa-Romeos, sunk low with their ears back, their heads and bodies parallel to the ground, their colours blurred. They look like completely different animals in the wild.'

I was struck by how soft these men were about animals which they were helping but who paid them no attention. Even Sangito was the same. When he came back from leave, he saw the dogs they'd released a month earlier come back through the camp, clobbering the dik-dik and having the time of their lives. 'They headed over there,' he said, 'and they didn't even stop and say hello to me.' He'd been with them for something like twelve years, and he was slightly sad that they hadn't even given him the time of day.

The next morning we flew back to the enclosures for the dogs' release. The two that had been collared had settled down. The male dogs were staring out of the enclosure towards a goat carcass tied to a nearby tree. That was what would greet them, their first taste of freedom. But first Tony let the two females out. As soon as I saw them reach the carcass, I had to push open the door of the male dogs' enclosure. Letting them free was a big thing for me. I was fascinated to see how they would react to their new-found freedom. Nina the elephant had been in a *boma* for about seven weeks so that she could get acclimatised to the area, but even so when we opened the gate she wouldn't leave and stayed put for another eight weeks. I couldn't imagine these guys would be the same – a quick bellyful of goat and they'd be off.

As Tony opened the gate the females stood for a moment, staring at their free passage. When he clapped his hands, one of them moved forward as if unable to believe what was happening, then hopped out. The other followed quickly and they went straight to the goat. Meanwhile, the five males were dashing about their enclosure as if they knew something was about to happen. I slipped the bolt, pushed the gate open and stood back. They streamed out, heading straight to the carcass and ripping into it with little yaps and squeals. Immediately the two females retreated behind one of the enclosures, followed by the males. They ran round and round together before the males went back to the carcass.

Suddenly all hell broke loose. The males had turned on the old girl who had roamed outside their cage for so long. As she tried to get a share of the carcass, they attacked her. Without Tony's shouts to break the fight up, they would have killed her. 'They've been getting on so well through the wire. I really thought they would accept her,' he said. 'Look! She's going back for more.'

I was surprised that Tony had waded in so quickly, knowing that he'd probably now have to look after the old dog for the rest of her life. We watched as she approached, then shied away, nervous of the young males' reaction. Like us, she seemed not to understand why they didn't want her. Eventually, after hovering on the edge but not being given a look in, she retreated to be with the two young females who were still keeping their distance. Tony seemed confident that they would bond with the males eventually. 'It's too early to say whether splitting them up before release has worked better. Last time, when I put the two sexes together, they were under sedation. They all woke up together and just went, "Oh, there's more of us." I only had tabs on them for two months before the collars packed up, so I've no idea how long they stayed together. I was hoping that separating them would hype them up a bit and make them more doggified.'

At last, their bellies full, the males started to show some interest in the young females. They still wanted nothing to do with the old girl. Sangito thought that in captivity exchanging greetings with her through the wire had been one thing, but that as soon as they got out the fact that she wasn't part of their family group mattered.

'I'm sure it will settle down,' said Tony. 'The guys are brothers and the females are sisters. But this poor old thing doesn't have a friend in the bank so no one's going to accept her. Maybe it's because she's not a breeding female. We can treat her wounds and I'll move her back into camp. We've always tried to stick by pack rules. By introducing her into the mix, we've broken them. So what this has taught me is that you cannot under any circumstances deviate from those rules and expect them to get on.'

Meanwhile, the males were exhibiting new behaviour. All four of them were submitting to the dominant collared male, beginning to coalesce into the pack that they had previously never formed because of the apathy engendered by captivity. Three of those four began running as one at the boundary of the clearing in a way they hadn't done when they weren't free. Despite living with them, Sangito hadn't been sure until now which of the two collared dogs was the dominant one. In their first forty minutes of freedom, it had become obvious.

As we waited for the pack to cohere, Sangito, Freddie and Tony enticed the old girl into the empty male enclosure with the head of the goat. The males ran round and round the outside, chattering, while she still looked as if she wanted to join them. However, they had made it clear that there was no role for her in their lives. 'There's no room for sentimentality or anthropomorphic feeling with these guys when you're planning a release,' said Tony. 'It was lackadaisical thinking on my part to think that she'd integrate. Whether I separate the sexes next time will depend on the data I get when they're free. All I need to see to know that it's worked is a pregnant female in the group. The problem is the speed at which they travel. They can cover thirty kilometres in a morning.'

I felt so lucky to have played a part in setting these wild dogs free. The emotional attachment to them that I've had ever since I was a child was reinforced when I came to Mkomazi thirteen years ago and met Tony's first dogs. Yet, out of all the canines I've met, these were the least bothered by our human presence. They didn't wag their tails with the same sort of purpose. They didn't want to jump up and sniff, smell or lick, craving interaction – even Shaun's wolves did that. I miss that. They're not dogs in the sense that Mary, Tina and Arthur are. You wouldn't want to spend time in front of a fire with them, beautiful though they are. Even in the presence of wolves and coyotes I still thought I was among dogs, but these are definitely one step away from my little cockers or even the labrador. Despite my strong affection and long-term fascination with these animals, they haven't got the dogness that I'm used to, but they remain so special – particularly when you think how few of them there are.

22

For the Best

Dorset

*'I've been told I must behave as the pack leader . . .
and make our dogs know their place.'*

Over six months, I'd seen how our relationship with dogs has evolved from the moment, thousands of years ago, when wolves and man crossed the species barrier. Since then, we have established a unique relationship that has been of nothing but mutual benefit.

Meeting wolves and working dogs, learning something of the advances being made in psychological and medical research, hasn't changed the way I view dogs but I'm considerably more informed. I like dogs so much, and so much of my life at home revolves around Mary, Tina and Arthur and our other animals, that to put all that at arm's length and say I wanted to study the subject of dogs seriously didn't hold that long when I was confronted with an animal that I wanted to chuckle. I've always been a dog voyeur, and when I get the chance I'm still all over them like a cheap suit. My fear that I would find myself a lone bunny-hugger in a world of sensible people was not realised at all.

Everyone I met had a special relationship with their own dogs.

There are lots of reasons why the whole man–dog thing has worked so well for so long, but perhaps the biggest is less to do with nature and more to do with us. Maybe we are confusing the instincts of a pack animal with unconditional love, but the bottom line is that they make us feel good. And we love them, don't we? And perhaps that's the most important thing.

Looking at the way our relationship has developed in different ways has only reinforced my feelings for dogs. However, I do now look at Tina, Mary and Arthur and view their behaviour in a different way. Discovering how wolves operate such a tight pack structure, in which every member's role is clearly defined, and talking to experts who relate that pack behaviour to the way they treat their own dogs, has made me see that we're not going to solve Mary and Tina's battle for dominance by projecting human values on to what they do.

I've been told that I must behave as the pack leader, not as a bunny-hugging human being, and make our dogs know their place. As a result of that and what I've learned, I've been able to be tougher with them, ignoring them in the morning (though not Mary) for as long as I can and not making a fuss of them till they settle (rotten, that's the best bit). But however much I've learned, I realise that I have to find my own version of controlling them and try to stick to it.

334

We've listened to what the experts Jean, Sarah and Rosemary have had to say about our problem, as well as the views of our other dog-owning friends. We've talked of muzzling Tina, or keeping and exercising the cockers separately, or rehoming Tina temporarily or permanently.

Rosemary's advice hit us like a sledgehammer and we realised we'd have to do something. Here was a situation involving three dogs and three humans, and some decisive action needed to be taken. And since one of these humans is only eight years old, the lead must come from Philippa and me – or so you'd think.

But here's the thing.

We delayed making any firm decision until we moved back into the big house, still clinging to the hope that it might provide the answer to our problem. Sure enough, immediately after the move we didn't have another attack for two or three weeks, except for one tiny bout that I closed my eyes to. One photo shoot too many meant that once, as I was posing the dogs, Tina had a little go at Mary; but it didn't last. I instinctively dealt with it in a different way this time, whipping her under my arm and stroking her, making nothing of it. She seemed to respond well to that.

Our new kitchen occupies the ground floor of the house, the Aga's relit and the dogs had new baskets, Tina and Arthur in one corner and Mary in another (though she still gets to spend the night upstairs). The two cockers seemed much more relaxed in the bigger space, sticking like limpets to the heated floor. With three doors, there's no need to fight for the right to go out or come in first.

As if Tina had heard Rosemary's dire pronouncements, she was calm and kind, going to squat alongside Mary illicitly in a stable, peeing on the fresh bedding like two old women in a khazi together. They went out walking together, inexplicably without any trouble. At mealtimes, we made them all sit before they can have their food. This was another routine we'd started before and allowed to fall by the wayside. Tina became a different dog.

Mary seemed to be in a good place too. She even started to enjoy Arthur, forgetting to growl when he kissed her. Arthur was going from strength to strength, responding to training and even coming to me when I was riding Chester thanks to Rosemary's trick of throwing him the occasional treat and working with him on the 'heel' command.

For the time being, we just kept an eye on the cockers and hoped for the best. Whatever advice we had been given, there was no escaping the fact that it was our mess and we had to wear it as well as we could. A part of both Philippa and me suspected that peace might not reign forever, but for the moment we were all living in a state of happy denial.

We were lulled into security for two or three weeks, until, I suspect, the old patterns of territory between the dogs must have been re-established. Neither Philippa nor I noticed what, if anything, provoked Tina but she renewed her attacks on Mary with a ferocity we hadn't seen before. However we tried to distract her, Tina refused to take her eyes off Mary. Day in, day out, she'd be watching her every move and attacking her even when she was lying asleep in her basket. There was no question in our minds that this time Tina was acting with real intent. She drew blood each time, the bites on Mary's ears only millimetres away from her neck. One of us always waded in to haul Tina off but that only provoked Mary into attacking back. It was as if she was saying to us, 'That's right. You hold her and I'll bite her.'

The three of us were devastated. This was exactly what we had hoped had gone away for good. We still resisted the idea of sending Tina away, but didn't know what else to do. Our attempts to train her didn't sufficiently occupy her, her mind seemed fixed on one thing only - Mary. In desperation we consulted our vet. He prescribed doggie downers (dogadon, surely) that had been used with some success on other dogs. In Tina's case, they only seemed to intensify her rage. As a last resort, he offered Valium. We were appalled that this was what we had come to. We didn't want to live with some kind of zombie dog but felt we had to try anything. A couple of pills induced a drowsiness that we hated to see in the spirited little dog that we adored. Even then, through her haze, she still attacked Mary.

I was away filming in the Shetlands when Philippa

finally snapped. After yet another day of pulling the dogs apart and having being bitten twice on her arm, she decided enough was enough. By the time I got back, Tina was parked with friends of ours down the road. Philippa and Emily had taken Tina there together, both sobbing. Emily took Tina's bed so that she would have something she was familiar with, that would make her feel more at home.

We had to face facts. However much we might want the situation to improve, it wasn't going to. All of us were unhappy and Mary's life was in danger. Ever since the most recent attacks, she had been pretty shaky. We had to put a stop to this for good. Another conversation with Jean provided an answer, albeit it one that broke our hearts. Having twenty-two dogs of her own at the moment, she didn't have room for Tina, but she thought she did know a couple who might give her a good home. We had no qualms about how she would behave with anyone else. We knew from our own experience what a delightful dog she was without Mary as a distraction and rival. Philippa and I talked to a tearful Emily.

'We'll have to stop wondering where Tina is and what she's doing. We've got to remember that she's going to be in a good home where she'll be happy.'

But whatever we said, none of us could ignore the real heartache that we felt at the idea that we would probably never see Tina again. However much we had mentally engaged with the idea of her leaving us, this was one of the hardest things we'd had to face together. As Emily's toys came out of storage for the new house, out came all the photo albums stuffed with photos of her and Tina. There are photos of all three dogs all over the house. We couldn't just forget she ever existed.

Then, unprovoked and unexpected, Philippa's mother stepped into the breach. Brian and Lynne's dog-owning days ended when their children grew up and their last cocker, Poppy, died. They've been so busy since Brian's retirement, that although always happy to have Mary to stay now and then, neither of them particularly wanted a dog full-time. But family – and that includes the dogs – is so important to Lynne that when she saw how miserable we were and how gutted Emily was in particular, she realised they could provide the best solution by offering a home to Tina. We still can't believe her generosity and our luck.

Sad though we are that Tina isn't here to walk with us any more, we're happy knowing that she's living in clover, that we get regular news of her and we can visit her whenever we want. The tension in the house has understandably dissipated in her absence, since we're no longer on edge all the time, waiting for the next attack.

Of course, we all miss her – even though Mary must feel huge relief. We miss the bang of the cat flap as she burst into the house, her exuberance and the pleasure she takes in life. I miss her presence on walks, watching her run for joy and jump up with affection. Even Arthur has lost a best friend. Perhaps, when time has passed and we're more used to her absence, our next task will be to find him another.

Since we moved into the house, I've been lobbying for a terrier to deal with the rats – and to bring the dog numbers up. Emily and I would have any terrier, although Philippa won't have a Jack Russell – but never say never. Another dog will never be a replacement for Tina, but the dynamics of the family will be different. I hope we've learned what we need to know about managing our pack better. The daily routine of poo-picking, feeding, exercising, riding, picking horses' hooves is non-stop with all the animals we have now. As for the other animals? We've moved the chickens out of the garden into a new run and are getting a rooster. And we're hoping Jemima will foal next year. But one little terrier wouldn't make a difference. Would it?

Acknowledgments

Elements of this Work refer to the television programme 'Martin Clunes: One Man and His Dogs' an ITV Productions and Buffalo Pictures production for itv

The author would like to thank Fanny Blake, Siobhan Machin, Lisa Highton, Heather Rainbow, Bill Jones, Ian Leese, Kuz Randawa, Richard Ranken, my trophy bride Philippa and our saviours Lynne & Brian Braithwaite.

Picture Acknowledgments

Most of the photographs are from the author's collection.
Additional sources:
Joël Lacey/*Dogs Today*, p10 bottom.
Courtesy Jean Ormes, p11 top.
Jane Nowak, p17 bottom.
Lichfield/Getty Images, p18 bottom.
Kennel Club Picture Library, p22, p23 top left, right, and centre.
Geoff Moore/Rex Features, p23 bottom left.
Nicky Johnston, p28, 29 and 32.

Every reasonable effort has been made to trace copyright holders, but if there are any errors or omissions, Hodder & Stoughton will be pleased to insert the appropriate acknowledgement in any subsequent edition.

Martin Clunes is one of Britain's favourite actors, the star of *Doc Martin* and the voice of Kipper the dog. He lives in the west country with his family and their dogs.